Cook Yourself Happy

CAROLINE FLEMING

Cook Yourself Happy

The Danish Way

CAROLINE FLEMING

Photography by Lisa Linder

jacqui
small

DEDICATION

I dedicate this book to my beloved parents and my three children, Alexander, Josephine and Nicholas.
    My late mother was the first to hold my hand as we walked through nature, collecting produce. My late father was still alive for the majority of my recipe writing, always there to share ideas and good tips. Now he has very sadly joined my beloved mother in heaven. Not a day goes by when I don't miss them and wish they were here. My three beautiful children and I have so many precious memories of them. We will continue to keep their memories alive through the many generations to come with all the food we cook and eat and with all the love we have for each other.

First published in 2017 by
Jacqui Small
An imprint of The Quarto Group
74–77 White Lion Street
London N1 9PF

Text copyright © 2017 by Caroline Fleming
Photography, design and layout copyright © Jacqui Small 2017

The author's moral rights have been asserted.

Publisher: Jacqui Small
Senior Commissioning Editor: Fritha Saunders
Managing Editor: Emma Heyworth-Dunn
Design: CHD
Editor and Project Manager: Claire Wedderburn-Maxwell
Photographer: Lisa Linder
Food Stylist: Mikkel Karstad
Production: Maeve Healy

ISBN: 978-1-911127-28-4

A catalogue record for this book is available from the British Library.

2019 2018 2017
10 9 8 7 6 5 4 3 2 1

Printed in China

Quarto is the authority on a wide range of topics.
Quarto educates, entertains and enriches the lives of our readers – enthusiasts and lovers of hands-on living.
www.QuartoKnows.com

Contents

Introduction

As a child I would often spend time with my mother and grandmother outdoors. On weekends we would go foraging for mushrooms or blueberry picking. I remember sitting in the fields eating glorious, crunchy green peas, feeling the warm breeze on my face and loving the pea shells and scented air around me.

A favourite pastime was climbing up our cherry tree, losing track of the height as I searched for the next juicy cherry. I would sit there for hours, eating the luscious dark cherries until my tummy hurt; on one occasion I had to be taken down by the fire brigade because I climbed too high to be able to get down alone!

Another tradition was rolling down the enormous sand dunes of Skagen followed by a sumptuous feast of *fjord rejer* – mini baby prawns (shrimp). They seemed to take forever to peel, but it was always worth it for that very first bite.

Since I was a little girl, I just loved food. When other children may have asked for sausages or spaghetti, I wanted to have mackerel with tomato sauce and mayonnaise in an open Danish sandwich, or plain grilled (broiled) sardines with sea salt and lemon. I may also have asked for steamed mussels, baby prawns (shrimp) or warm smoked salmon – all so delicious and fragrant, eaten with a warm newly baked loaf of rye bread.

So many of the recipes here are based on dishes I loved as a child, traditional food that my parents and grandparents enjoyed, and ingredients merged with impressions from my travels around the world.

A Lifelong Love of Cooking

I have always loved cooking and I have always cooked. Cooking is very nostalgic and reminds me of my past, yet it also keeps me in the present and is a very mindful exercise. Cooking satisfies all my senses and it is a great way of showing love through the time spent thinking about – and preparing – food for the ones you care about. I put a lot of thought into developing each of my recipes. I think of my children, family and friends and the goodness I am preparing for them, and I think of my parents and grandparents and the love they poured into me through our meals and the special times spent together. In my family, even when we are eating we are talking about the next meal. We are enjoying it, dreaming about it and discussing it at great length. Cooking and the results are (for me) 'love' that you can taste, smell and touch – all a big part, I think, of making us the happiest people.

Denmark – A Very Special Country

Denmark used to include Norway (1814) and Iceland (1944), and still holds within its kingdom The Faroe Islands and Greenland, making it a major northern European cultural community and land owner.

Denmark is made up of hundreds of islands, surrounding most people with beaches and water, hence it has a very passionate fishing culture. I don't think I know any child born in Denmark who didn't go crabbing every summer, or spend time on a boat with a parent or grandparent either fishing or trawling.

The boat and camping culture are still at large to this day, and most Danes have a summer house or *kolonihavehus* – a garden community chalet. Danes love their country, and travel in the holidays around these glorious islands via car, caravan or boat. There are many Danes who never really travel outside of Denmark, as they feel they have everything they need at home.

The seasons in Denmark are very defined. There is almost always snow in winter, and cross-country skiers enjoy dashing through the woods. In spring, as the buds blossom, the home/street vendors start selling their home-grown produce from small stalls on the street, trusting each buyer to put their payment into little padlocked boxes.

The summers in Denmark can be very warm, sunny and glorious, but they never last very long. When it is hot and the sun is shining, there isn't a more gorgeous place to be on the planet. The peas and cherries are so sweet; apple trees, pear trees, plum trees and cherry trees line most streets. It is thought that the more cherries we harvest from our gardens, the colder the coming winter will be.

Harvest time is a glorious reminder that summer has once again succeeded in her riches. The scent of barbecues fills the air daily, everywhere you go, as the pretty fishing boats, now constantly at sea, collect the amazing seafood we are so lucky to have access to throughout the year. At the end of the day, every day, it's time to *hygge* with the people you love. Luckily that often entails lots of yummy things to eat…

Adopting a Danish Way of Life

Hygge doesn't translate exactly, but roughly means a feeling of 'cosiness'. For us Danes, this means always being in a warm and cosy environment, being safe and secure as a child, knowing you are loved and supported unconditionally, never working too hard or too many hours, thereby never sacrificing time with your family, which comes first in our world.

Hygge is now becoming a part of life outside of Denmark, the power of its meaning slowly moving into homes across the globe. Everyone is waking up to the fact that life is short. It is about living life to the fullest and being as happy as you can. As a consequence of this attitude to life, food has also become much more

important and dishes have developed stronger meanings and importance through time.

Seasonal Eating

For most Danes December is a very important month for food. We go to fabulous 'Christmas lunches' hosted by work, friends or family. To start, there are open sandwiches topped with fish, such as herrings, followed by warm toppings such as *frikadeller* (meatballs), *leverpostej* (liver pâté) or *flæskesteg* (roast pork). These 'lunches' start around 6pm and go on well into the night. With the beer and aquavit flowing freely all evening, the end result is often minimal recollection of conversation!

It's not just at Christmas that we celebrate with food, such as *flæskesteg* (roast pork), or Christmas duck. In many homes, and without fail in my grandparents' house, New Year's Eve is always celebrated with baked or steamed cod with mustard sauce and beetroot.

Life is renewed, as decreed in the Bible, at Easter, when lamb is very popular on the menu. A great celebratory dish is my sticky honey and mustard marinated slow-cooked leg of lamb or the delicious lamb meatballs with parsley, olives, red (bell) peppers and feta.

Summer is all about enjoying what the season has to offer in abundance: fresh pea soup with mint, fragrant beetroot with stirred salted butter, lumpfish roe with red onion and crème fraîche and monkey food fruit salad, to name just a few favourites.

With the arrival of the crunchy, crispy sounds of leaves crackling under your feet in autumn, it's time to start lighting the fires again, and even more candles than you would normally light on a daily basis. This is also the time that I find myself going into a more

intense baking mode... As we leave the warmth behind, I find that baking fills the house with a warm sensation and the to-die-for scent of cosy, *hyggelige* baked goods – cinnamon buns, vanilla and oat cookies and Danish birthday buns are all the smell of home. I believe in the old Danish saying that although 'out is good, home is best'.

A Wealth of Produce

Go into a typical Danish fishmonger, and the exquisite smells will make your mouth water. Or visit a Danish butcher, where there will be a gorgeous and clean aroma of smoked delicatessen meats. It makes for a great business as you always end up buying many more things than on your shopping list... And all these yummies are, in fact, pretty easy to make at home, too.

The Danes are also major cheese farmers. A large proportion of my food when I was growing up comprised cheese on bread with a thick layer of butter and a glass of milk. It is rare now for people outside of Denmark to give their child such a start to the day. We still enjoy enormously many different dairy products, and have also grown to love more easily digestible alternatives to traditional Danish cheeses, such as feta. In Danish supermarkets, in the cheese section, there will always be a few varieties of feta, in little pots of brine or oil, some seasoned with herbs, and I find this to be a wonderful substitute to a normal cow's milk cheese.

I had presumed our national dish was *flæskesteg* (roast pork), which many people have on Christmas Day, but in fact *stegt flæsk* (crispy fried pork slices) won that competition. Our national dish is just an extraordinary combination of Danish flavours. The very salty *flæsk*, which is similar to bacon but a little more

fatty, is cooked in the oven to maximum crunchiness. It is served with warm new Danish potatoes, a creamy parsley sauce, pickled beetroot and cucumber. It is both salty and sweet, creamy and mild, hard and soft, crunchy and smooth, cold and warm, and so completely addictive that it is nearly impossible to stop eating it.

Cooking Wholesome Food the Danish Way

For me it is so important to nourish your heart, mind, body and soul. I am very sensitive to different foods and feel instantaneously the effects of what I eat and how I look after myself. I believe that we are what we eat! Having grown up with a typical, rich Danish diet, my adult years have taught me to be more sensitive to how I feel with each meal I have.

Working as a model and then as a TV presenter, needing high levels of energy for long days, while maintaining glowing skin and a feeling of wellbeing in very demanding times, were the inspiration behind me wanting to learn more about how the foods we eat affect how we feel.

I love food, and like many people, I want to be able to 'have my cake and eat it'. I have what I enjoy – whether bacon, burgers or cakes – but always in moderation and in a balanced diet with plenty of good, nutritious food. I have taught myself to make a wealth of wonderful dishes with the right balance of the good alkaline ingredients to neutralize the more acidic ingredients, as I find that a more alkaline way of living is best in terms of all-round good health.

Unless it's processed, I don't believe there are any really 'bad' foods. Enjoy everything – fat, sugar, carbs... just do it all in moderation and find the right and healthy balance of foods for you. Be proud of loving food – it's our fuel, and it's a pleasure, so take pride in it, and eat well so you feel great and stay healthy.

My Favourite Foods

I would much prefer to go food shopping than shopping for clothes any day of the week – to me it really is a treat to go and get the groceries.

I would, for example, not want to live without a simple ingredient like pink Himalayan salt, which, after I learned about its extraordinary health benefits, became a daily handbag accessory. It is extremely rich in unpolluted minerals, and many people use it as a powerful antioxidant to remove harmful toxins. The most important fact to me is that pink Himalayan salt is an incredibly alkaline ingredient, and I believe it helps me to neutralize the harmful acidic build-up caused by excessive consumption of alcohol, coffee, sugar, meats and dairy products to name a few.

I wish I could grow my own lemons, avocados and cucumbers at home, as these three ingredients are consumed every day in my house. As a child, I would often ask my mother for half a peeled cucumber and some celery salt to dip it in. My children ask for the same, or a plate of avocado with pink Himalayan salt, drizzled with oil and fresh lemon juice.

Kale is another favourite ingredient of mine – the forgotten cabbage is now back with a vengeance! Kale has always been used in Danish cooking, and was in fact one of my great grandmother's favourite ingredients. She would cook it nearly every day, whether creamed or sautéed as a side dish, or cooked in a soup or stew.

Kale is so versatile. I often serve my kale and quinoa salad as a side dish to balance heavier meat dishes. I also love kale and bacon soup in the colder months, and my kale chips are a perfect movie snack alternative to popcorn.

I could eat salmon for breakfast, lunch and dinner, all day, every day. Fresh grilled (broiled) salmon, gravadlax, warm smoked salmon, salmon Caesar salad or salmon eaten straight out of the river after a fishing trip, Scout style, whether in Denmark, Sweden, Ireland or Scotland, although I will also bring some wasabi and soy sauce on these excursions, and my treasured Japanese knife.

The wise men have always said that 'an apple a day keeps the doctor away', and I swear by this statement as apples have such great anti-fungal properties. I like to simply cut an apple into boats and sprinkle it with cinnamon, or they are delicious baked with marzipan and raisins. An apple really is a sensational ingredient – one I would not want to live without – and makes one of the most simple, tasty and healthy snacks around.

How I Like to Eat

I eat often during the day, always beginning with breakfast quite soon after I wake up. I am as happy with smoked pheasant and scrambled eggs as I am with a cinnamon bun, and of course lots of milky coffee.

I really enjoy salads for lunch, for example the smoked mackerel salad, or my father's delicious chicken and celery salad. Soups are also fantastic in my opinion. If you want something satisfying, whip up a batch of beetroot (beet) soup with baked feta or the Jerusalem artichoke and truffle soup. These are also perfect as a starter for dinner, or served in an enormous bowl as a main course with freshly baked rye bread and 'tooth butter', which we Danes adore.

In fact, I'm unsure where we Danes would be without our open sandwich, it's become so ingrained in our

14 culture, it's like the air we breathe, it's the type of body petrol we cannot be without.

For dinner I have what my body wants and needs that day. It can be a light and fruity curry, or my delicious poussin casserole, which is even better the day after it is made. Also, about once a month, I want red meat, either steak tartar or rib of beef with a delicious salad or root vegetables.

Experiment with the Foods You Enjoy

For all my recipes, there are always great alternatives, and it's my opinion that there is no right or wrong way to cook something. One seed can be replaced with another, red meat can be replaced with fish or chicken, and I often replace normal flour with oats, almonds and coconut ... somehow it just all works.

My children also enjoy adapting age-old family recipes – my daughter, Josephine, has created her take on the traditional *frikadeller* (meatballs) recipe, using turkey rather than pork, as it's easier to digest but just as tasty.

I love the fact that so many recipes have passed down through the generations, perfected and tweaked with each set of hands that they have passed through. These recipes are wonderful reminders of times past in a very fast-changing world. Now they are in my hands and with the benefit of all of my knowledge of health and wellness, I, too, have tweaked them for this generation of food lovers.

Cooking Is My Greatest Pleasure

The kitchen has always been where my family congregates. In times of happiness or sadness, cooking is our greatest indulgence and passion. There is a great democracy in the kitchen – you work as a team for a common goal – you can have difficult conversations, you can laugh, you can argue, all over a hot stove or a chopping board. Some of my most important conversations have taken place in the heart of my home. And if I'm ever unsure about a recipe or life, I just phone home to my 92-year-old grandmother.

In my family, the most precious heirlooms are from the kitchen. I was recently given my grandmother's favourite cooking pot (see page 256). I have watched this in action all my life, and felt a little melancholy being given it, but my grandmother felt it was time to rehome the pot with me. I hope she will have many tasty meals cooked by me in this treasured pot.

My father was a connoisseur like no other, and has left behind such a legacy. Whenever he cooked, which was a daily passion, we all knew we were in for a treat. His dishes are the ones I make all the time: especially his spaghetti with tuna fish sauce or the incredible yet very simple roast chicken with pickled cucumber, which he had every year on his birthday.

I also recently rediscovered my mother's food bread recipe, which was 'lost' for almost 30 years, and which I now make every couple of weeks. The magic surrounding family recipes passed down through the generations is next to none – find them, make them and treasure them always.

Quite simply, cooking is my favourite pastime, my greatest passion, and I hope to inspire you to love cooking too. To cook for my family and to cook for my friends is as gratifying to me as embracing my loved ones. To cook with them is magic. The times I spend in my kitchen with my children are my greatest pleasures – the food preparation, baking and eating together is such a 'glue' in our lives, it's the happiest times spent together, full of cosiness and *hygge*.

Chapter One

Light Meals
to Enjoy Any Time

Gravad Laks med Rævesovs

GRAVADLAX WITH 'SAUCE OF THE FOX'

SERVES 16 AS A STARTER

This dish has always been very popular in my family, especially because my mother's family are from Sweden, where this originates. The sweet and clean-tasting, fresh but salty taste of gravadlax is one of the oldest flavours of Scandinavia, and is one of our most favoured delicacies. Infused with dill, a very popular herb in Denmark, this is a dish that is easy to prepare anywhere you can buy fresh salmon, although you will need to allow two days for curing.

FOR THE GRAVADLAX

1 whole fresh salmon fillet, about
    1kg (2¼lb), skin on, bones removed
    (make sure it is sushi-quality salmon
    or freeze the fish first for 24 hours
    to make sure it can be eaten raw)
200g (7oz/1 cup) sea salt
100g (3½oz/½ cup) raw cane sugar
1 tbsp crushed black peppercorns
4 large bunches of dill (or 8 tbsp
    dried dill)

Place the salmon in a shallow ceramic fish dish or glass dish. Mix together the salt, sugar and peppercorns and spread over the fleshy side of the fish. Then spread the dill over the top of the fish and press it down. Cover the fish with clingfilm (plastic wrap), then place a heavy weight on top of the fish – you can use a heavy dish, full jam (jelly) jars or a sealable bag with water. Put the salmon in the fridge and leave for 2 days to cure.

FOR THE 'SAUCE OF THE FOX'

4 tbsp Swedish mustard or sweet
    mustard (or 2 tbsp mustard and
    2 tbsp honey)
2 tbsp Dijon mustard
2 tbsp brown sugar
2 tbsp white wine vinegar or
    apple cider vinegar
1 small tsp salt
2 tbsp chopped dill
50–100ml (2–3½fl oz/
    scant ¼–½ cup) grapeseed oil

The salmon will be ready to eat after 48 hours of curing. Remove the salt cure and rinse the fish under cold running water. Pat dry with kitchen towel and slice thinly.

Mix together all the ingredients for the sauce. Taste and season with extra salt and pepper if you like.

Serve the salmon with freshly baked bread and butter together with the sauce and some extra dill sprinkled on top.

TO SERVE

buttered rye bread (see page 208)
dill, to garnish

TIPS

— Ask the fishmonger to remove the bones for you.
— When the salmon is finished, my Auntie Beagle removes the scales and cuts the fish skin into pieces, then fries it up with a little olive oil and a little extra salt sprinkled on top to make salmon scratchings – absolutely delicious.

Varmrøget Laks med Syltede Agurker

WARM SMOKED SALMON WITH PICKLED CUCUMBER

SERVES 4

FOR THE SALMON

1 whole side of fresh raw salmon, about 500g (1lb 2oz)
½ tsp pink Himalayan salt or sea salt
2 tbsp olive oil
1 tbsp citrus herb mix

FOR THE PICKLED CUCUMBER

1 cucumber
2 tbsp pink Himalayan salt or sea salt
150ml (5fl oz/⅔ cup) water
200ml (7fl oz/generous ¾ cup) white wine vinegar
1 tbsp raw cane sugar
16 whole red peppercorns
½ tsp mustard seeds
4 cloves
1 tbsp finely chopped dill

TO GARNISH

dill

Like *fiskefrikadeller* (fish balls, see page 158), warm smoked salmon is found on every fish counter near most harbours across Denmark. It is so easy to take home and heat, the fat melting into the flesh, traditionally eaten with freshly baked and buttered rye bread. Sadly, those Danish fish counters are not found all over the world, so this is one way to make warm smoked salmon at home. The flavour is delicately smokey, creamy and so good!

In Denmark, we typically love to eat lightly smoked salmon, mackerel, eel and pheasant breast (see page 31). As fish and meat smokers are relatively easy to find nowadays online, and aren't too expensive, it's well worth investing in one. Using apple wood chips is the icing on the cake.

First prepare the pickled cucumber. Cut the cucumber into very thin slices and place in a flat glass or ceramic serving dish. Sprinkle over the salt and leave for 30 minutes. Now mix the rest of the pickled cucumber ingredients together and pour over the cucumber slices. Leave to marinate for at least 1 hour.

Place the fish in a glass or ceramic dish. Mix together the salt, olive oil and citrus herb mix and spread over the top of the salmon. Leave to marinate for 30 minutes.

Prepare the smoker according to the manufacturer's instructions (see also Tips below) and smoke the salmon for 25 minutes.

Serve the warm smoked salmon with the pickled cucumber on the side, and scatter with dill.

TIPS

— I like to use apple wood chips in my smoker as I think it makes the salmon taste more delicious, and the scent of the fish cooking over the wood chips is quite fabulous.
— The pickled cucumber also works well with a liver pâté open sandwich (see page 64) or my lamb meatballs (see page 132).

Avocado med Caviar

AVOCADO WITH CAVIAR

SERVES 4

2 ripe yet firm avocados
1 tbsp chia oil
1 tsp sea salt
lemon juice
125g (4½oz/½ cup) caviar
1 tsp toasted sesame seeds

Denmark is a super-cool place, and is currently having its shining moment, especially where the arts, culture and food are concerned. Noma, in Copenhagen, was voted the best restaurant in the world for several years running, and avant-garde chefs are emerging left, right and centre. Food combos are changing in this incredible and unique time. This is one of my absolute favourite combinations, inspired by a fantastic chef and dear friend of mine, Bo Bech.

Peel the avocados, cut in half and remove and discard the stones, then cut into thin slices.

Divide the avocado slices between 4 plates and rub each slice with a little chia oil, then sprinkle each with a little sea salt and lastly add a dab of lemon juice to each slice. Put in the fridge for 30 minutes to chill.

Remove the avocado from the fridge and divide the caviar between each plate, placing it delicately on the avocado. Sprinkle over the sesame seeds and serve immediately.

Torskerognsmousse

COD ROE MOUSSE

SERVES 6–8

FOR THE COE ROE MOUSSE
400g (14oz) cod roe
juice of 1 lemon
1 tbsp curry powder
¼ tsp smoked paprika
1 tsp pink Himalayan salt or sea salt
2 tbsp mayonnaise
½ tsp Dijon mustard

TO SERVE
rye bread (see page 208)
butter
tarragon, to garnish
lemon quarters

On every fish counter, in season, the roes of cod are piled high – however, it's not just in season that we consume cod roe. It is a popular topping for Danish children's packed lunches all year round, often served very simply on a piece of rye bread with remoulade (see page 158) and fried crispy onions on top.

My father was a superstar at making this dish, his version tasting better than anyone else's. In my family, we have enjoyed this delicious mousse for years, usually as a starter for the evening meal.

In a bowl, mix all the ingredients for the mousse together until smooth, then put into the fridge to cool for at least an hour.

When ready to serve, toast very thin slices of rye bread, spread with butter and top with the mousse. Sprinkle over a few tarragon leaves and serve with lemon quarters to squeeze over.

Stenbiderrogn med Rødløg og Crème Fraîche

LUMPFISH ROE WITH RED ONION
AND CRÈME FRAîCHE

SERVES 3–4

250g (9oz/1 cup) fresh (or frozen)
   lumpfish roe
100ml (3½fl oz/scant ½ cup)
   crème fraîche
½ red onion, very finely chopped
½ lemon, cut into wedges
thin slices of bread, toasted
sea salt and freshly ground pepper,
   to taste

There is a song called '*Sommer og Sol*', meaning 'Summer and Sun', by Birthe Kjær… in fact there are countless and rather fabulously 'happy-go-lucky' Danish songs. These songs bring with them an incredible feeling deep inside regardless of the season – for example, when it rains, playing these songs brings out the sunshine inside. This is one of those dishes that makes my family feel good – it's a sign that summer is once again on its way.

   Lumpfish roe, also known as Swedish caviar or lumpsucker roe or caviar, is a real treat, a rare delicacy to be consumed for the short time it is in season. If you can't source lumpfish roe then you can use salmon roe instead.

Defrost the lumpfish roe if required.

Put each of the ingredients into individual bowls. Place everything on the table so everyone can help themselves to their own portion.

Traditionally this is eaten rather like caviar, with the roe, crème fraîche and red onion on the plate, a little lemon juice squeezed onto the roe, and the toast on the side. Add a sprinkle of salt and pepper to taste.

Rejecocktail med Grønkålschips

PRAWN (SHRIMP) AND AVOCADO
COCKTAIL WITH KALE CHIPS

SERVES 6–8

FOR THE KALE CHIPS
large bunch of curly kale, about 250g
    (9oz/3½ cups) stalks discarded,
    leaves torn into bite-sized pieces
large drizzle of olive oil
pink Himalayan salt or sea salt

FOR THE PRAWN (SHRIMP)
AND AVOCADO COCKTAIL
2 little gem lettuces
2 tbsp olive oil
1 clove of garlic, finely chopped
10 cherry tomatoes, finely chopped
500g (1lb 2oz) fresh prawns (shrimp),
    prawns (shrimp) in brine, or frozen
    prawns (shrimp), defrosted
juice of ½ lemon
1 tbsp chopped parsley, plus extra
    to garnish
1 avocado, finely diced
½ tsp pink Himalayan salt or sea salt
ground black pepper

In Denmark there are only a few special nights when darkness never really comes. Long summer days and even longer summer nights are never complete without some kind of seafood dish. Prawns (shrimp) come in so many different sizes, and the tiny fjord prawns (shrimp) are a family favourite, although peeling them takes an age compared with how quick they are to devour. The small prawns (shrimp) can be used here, but I find it just as delicious using normal-sized ones, or another kind of shellfish.

Preheat the oven to 200°C/400°F/gas mark 6.

To make the kale chips, drizzle the kale with olive oil and add a good pinch of salt. Massage well with your hands so the kale is coated evenly.

Put the kale into an ovenproof dish and bake for 15–20 minutes, checking after 15 minutes to make sure it doesn't burn. Once the kale is nice and crispy, transfer onto some kitchen towel and leave to cool – the kale will become even more crispy.

To make the prawn (shrimp) and avocado cocktail, cut off the ends of the lettuce stalks and discard, separate the leaves and wash and dry well.

Heat the olive oil in a frying pan (skillet), add the garlic and gently fry for a couple of minutes, then add the chopped tomatoes and cook for another 2 minutes.

Add the prawns (shrimp) and fry for another 2 minutes, then squeeze over the lemon juice and stir well. Lastly add the parsley and avocado. Season with salt and black pepper.

Remove from the heat, place in the little gem lettuce leaf cups, sprinkle with a little extra parsley and serve immediately with the kale chips on the side.

Røget Fasanbryst med Røræg

SMOKED PHEASANT BREAST WITH SCRAMBLED EGGS

SERVES 4

FOR THE SMOKED PHEASANT BREAST
2 pheasant breasts, about 150g (5½oz)
    total weight
2 tbsp olive oil
1 tsp pink Himalayan salt or smoked salt
1 tsp citrus herb seasoning

FOR THE TOMATO SAUCE
4 tbsp olive oil
1 small yellow onion, finely chopped
1 tsp tomato purée (paste)
16 cherry tomatoes, finely chopped
¼ tsp salt

FOR THE SCRAMBLED EGGS
12 eggs
¼ tsp pink Himalayan salt or sea salt
¼ tsp dried chilli flakes
1 tbsp chives
2 tbsp olive oil

TO SERVE
cress, to garnish
rye bread (see page 208)

Breakfast at home in Denmark growing up would not be the same without a regular serving of cold smoked pheasant breast. I have intense cravings for this if I go without it for more than a few months. It is a great alternative to bacon because of the wonderful light, smoky flavour, and is also incredibly delicious on top of an open sandwich with liver pâté – aka the vet's midnight food (see page 64).

About 20 years ago, in the kitchen of a Danish friend, I had an amazing experience when Dustin Hoffman taught me how to mix 12 egg whites, one egg yolk and two tablespoons of chives to make the tastiest scrambled eggs ever!

Put the pheasant breasts into a glass or ceramic bowl, drizzle over the olive oil and sprinkle over the salt and citrus herb seasoning. Leave to marinate for 30 minutes.

Prepare your smoker according to the manufacturer's instructions (I like to use wood chips in mine) and smoke the pheasant for 20–30 minutes.

To make the tomato sauce, heat the olive oil in a frying pan (skillet) and add the onion. Fry gently for 1 minute, then add the tomato purée (paste) and cook for another minute. Add the cherry tomatoes and the salt and simmer for 15 minutes. Transfer to a blender or food processor and blend until smooth.

To make the scrambled eggs, separate the egg whites and yolks, then put all 12 whites but only 4 yolks into a mixing bowl. Beat the eggs with the salt, chilli flakes and chives. Heat the oil in a saucepan, add the beaten eggs and cook, stirring, until your eggs are scrambled to your desired consistency.

Serve the scrambled eggs with the smoked pheasant breast, a sprinkle of cress on top, a good dollop of tomato sauce on the side and warm freshly baked rye bread.

Rørt Tartar

STEAK TARTARE

SERVES 6

FOR THE TARTARE

900g (2lb) minced (ground), or even
  better scraped or very finely chopped
  fillet steak (tell your butcher that it's
  for steak tartare to be eaten raw)
1 tsp pink Himalayan salt or sea salt
4 tbsp olive oil
1 small onion, very finely chopped
  or grated
10 small cornichons, very finely chopped
20–30 capers, very finely chopped
1–2 tbsp Dijon mustard
3 tbsp truffle oil (optional)
10 drops of Tabasco (optional)
4 squirts of Worcester sauce
2 eggs (optional)
1 tsp fresh horseradish, very finely
  chopped

FOR THE POTATO STICKS

4 large potatoes, washed well but
  not peeled
100ml (3½fl oz/scant ½ cup) olive oil
1 tsp finely chopped rosemary
½ tsp pink Himalayan salt or sea salt

TO SERVE

6 egg yolks
chopped chives, to garnish
fresh horseradish, grated, to garnish

There are so many fantastic ways to make steak tartare, and how I create mine depends on my mood and the season. This particular variation works well both in summer and winter. For those of you who don't like to eat raw meat, once mixed, the steak can be gently fried.

Preheat the oven to 200°C/400°F/gas mark 6.

First make the tartare. Put the minced (ground), scraped or chopped fillet steak into a large mixing bowl and add the salt.

Heat the olive oil in a small frying pan (skillet) and add the onion. Gently fry for a couple of minutes, then add to the meat and mix well. Now add all the remaining tartare ingredients and mix well using your hands, literally kneading the ingredients together.

Divide the tartare into 6 portions and scatter in a pile on a plate. Leave in the fridge until ready to serve.

Cut the potatoes into thick sticks. Massage the oil, rosemary and salt into the potato sticks then spread them out in an ovenproof dish. Bake in the oven for 45 minutes until golden and crispy, shaking occasionally to turn.

Place the steak tartare on a plate and top with an egg yolk, then sprinkle with chives and grated horseradish. Serve with the hot potato sticks on the side. If you prefer, the tartare is also delicious with freshly baked rye bread.

Chapter Two

Soups and
Open Sandwiches

Jordskokkesuppe med Trøffel

JERUSALEM ARTICHOKE AND TRUFFLE SOUP
WITH RYE BREAD CROUTONS

SERVES 6

FOR THE SOUP

600g (1lb 5oz) Jerusalem artichokes

3 tbsp olive oil

1 red onion, chopped

8 rashers (slices) of smoked streaky
   bacon, chopped

1 litre (1¾ pints/4 cups) chicken stock
   or water

½ tsp salt

FOR THE CROUTONS

4 tbsp olive oil

1 clove of garlic, crushed

4 thick slices of rye bread (see page
   208), or other bread, cut into strips

½ tsp pink Himalayan salt or sea salt

white truffle oil, to drizzle

TO SERVE

4 rashers (slices) of smoked streaky
   bacon

2 tbsp finely chopped parsley

4 tbsp white truffle oil

I remember so clearly the first time I tasted this soup. My Danish friend Søren had just serenaded us on the piano in Blakes Hotel, whereafter our friend Nikolaos ordered Blake's version of this dish. The flavour made such a huge impact on my taste buds that I have played around lots with this fabulous root vegetable. It's completely unique and for me a much loved flavour of winter. We Danes also adore our bacon and use 'any excuse' we can to add it to a dish.

Wash the Jerusalem artichokes well, then scrape off the thin outside layer with a kitchen knife. Cut the artichokes into thin slices and soak in water for 20 minutes, then drain.

Heat the olive oil in a large saucepan. Add the onion and fry for a few minutes to soften, then add the chopped bacon and fry for another couple of minutes. Next add the Jerusalem artichokes and pour in the stock. Bring to a gentle boil, add the salt, and simmer for 20 minutes.

While the soup is simmering, in a frying pan (skillet), heat the olive oil for the croutons and gently fry the garlic. Add the rye bread strips and sauté for about 5 minutes. Sprinkle with salt, then drain on kitchen towel until cooled and crispy. Just before serving, drizzle them with the truffle oil.

In another frying pan (skillet), fry the 4 rashers (slices) of bacon until crispy, then remove from the pan, drain on kitchen towel and chop.

Remove the soup from the heat, pour into a blender or food processor and blend to the desired consistency.

Serve the soup in soup bowls with the bacon and chopped parsley sprinkled on top. Finally drizzle each soup bowl with a little extra truffle oil and serve the rye bread croutons on top or on the side.

Ærtesuppe
PEA AND MINT SOUP

SERVES 6–8

FOR THE SOUP

2 tbsp olive oil

1 clove of garlic, crushed

1 red onion, finely chopped

20 mint leaves, torn

1 tsp pink Himalayan salt or sea salt

800ml (1½ pints/3⅓ cups) vegetable
   stock

800g (1lb 12oz/5 cups) fresh or
   frozen peas

6 rashers (slices) of streaky bacon
   (optional)

I still to this day dream of getting lost in Danish pea fields. We used to sit there for hours, opening the pods and eating peas by the hundred, the scent lingering so deeply in my memory bank. Although those days are long behind me, one of the first things I do when I go to Denmark for my summer holiday is to buy a big bag of fresh peas from one of the many local street vendors.

You can still find these vendors selling peas from little stands outside their houses in the summer months – it's rather magical when you drive through small villages and towns and come home with fresh strawberries, raspberries, cherries, new potatoes, carrots, kale, tomatoes, cucumbers and peas, all bought locally. It is so important nowadays to support your local farmers who take such great care and pride in their produce, ensuring that it's natural without adding any harmful additives.

Heat the olive oil in a large saucepan and add the garlic and onion. Fry for 2 minutes, then add the mint, salt and stock and bring to the boil. Simmer for 5 minutes, then add the peas and simmer for another 5 minutes.

Meanwhile, fry the bacon (if using) in a frying pan (skillet) until crispy, then remove from the pan and drain on kitchen towel.

In a blender or food processor, blend the soup until smooth then serve in deep soup bowls with the bacon. Or leave it unblended and serve it as it is ... which I occasionally prefer.

NOTE
— This is also absolutely delicious with fried crayfish tails when they are in season.

Svampesuppe

MUSHROOM SOUP

SERVES 4–6

FOR THE SOUP
1 whole garlic bulb
2 tbsp olive oil
1 white onion, finely chopped
200g (7oz) white button mushrooms, quartered
200g (7oz) brown button mushrooms, quartered
200g (7oz) Portobello mushrooms, cut into chunks
600ml (1 pint/2½ cups) vegetable stock
½ tsp salt
4 tbsp refined Japanese sake

FOR THE RYE BREAD CROUTONS
4 slices of rye bread (see page 208)
4–6 tbsp freshly grated Gruyère or Parmesan cheese
drizzle of truffle oil

TO SERVE
2 tbsp finely chopped parsley

I don't know what it is about mushrooms, but I just love them – the extraordinary texture, the gush of flavour and the often-funny shapes. As children, my sister and I would often persuade our father to take us to London for the weekend. Our first stop was Drones for lunch, where we devoured fried potato skins with crème fraîche and chives. Dinner would most often be Italian, where I would have wild mushrooms sautéed with garlic and parsley as a starter, and then again as a main course! This soup is a replica of that dish, but on another canvas.

Preheat the oven to 200°C/400°F/gas mark 6.

Cut the whole garlic bulb in half horizontally, place in a small oven-proof dish and roast in the oven for 45 minutes.

Heat the olive oil in a large saucepan, then add the onion and gently fry for a couple of minutes. Add the mushrooms and gently fry for a few more minutes, stirring, then squeeze in the roasted garlic pieces, discarding the skin of the garlic. Add the stock and salt and bring to the boil, then turn down the heat and simmer for 20 minutes.

Meanwhile, make the croutons. Cut the rye bread into chunks, place on a baking tray (sheet) and bake in the oven for 20 minutes.

When the soup is cooked, add the sake, stir well and turn off the heat. You can either serve the soup as it is, or transfer to a food processor or blender and blend until smooth.

To finish the croutons, preheat the grill (broiler). Sprinkle the grated cheese over the top, top with a drizzle of truffle oil and grill (broil) for 2 minutes until the cheese is bubbling. This soup is like a mushroom version of a classic gratinated onion soup.

To serve, divide the soup between 4–6 bowls, sprinkle over the chopped parsley and top with the croutons.

Rødbedesuppe med Bagt Feta

BEETROOT (BEET) SOUP WITH BAKED FETA

SERVES 6–8

FOR THE SOUP
400g (14oz) beetroot (beets)

2 tbsp olive oil

1 small red onion, roughly chopped

1 small clove of garlic, chopped

1–1.5 litres (1¾–2¾ pints/4–6 cups) beef
   or vegetable stock or water, depending
   on how thick you like your soup

½ tsp pink Himalayan salt or sea salt

1 tbsp apple cider vinegar

FOR THE BAKED FETA
200g (7oz) salted feta cheese

20g (¾oz) red (bell) pepper,
   finely chopped

20g (¾oz) green (bell) pepper,
   finely chopped

20g (¾oz) red onion, finely chopped

2 tbsp olive oil

Beetroot (beets), when really ripe, can be as sweet as blackcurrant cordial. I absolutely adore them, whether raw as spaghetti, pickled and served on an open sandwich with liver pâté (see page 64), or in a soup like this, with salty baked feta on top.

Nothing is quite as satisfying as pulling beetroot (beets) out of the ground with my children, the feeling when the earth around falls softly away, washing and then cooking with them. We ate so many beetroot as children that it would at times turn our waters deep purple! This soup resembles the Russian Borscht, but is much richer and fuller in flavour – enjoy.

Preheat the oven to 200°C/400°F/gas mark 6.

To make the soup, first wash the beetroot (beets), then cook whole or chop into chunks – it's best to wear gloves when doing this so your hands won't be stained purple.

In a large, deep saucepan, heat the olive oil and then add the onion and garlic and fry for 1 minute. Next add the chopped beetroot (beets), beef stock, salt and apple cider vinegar and simmer for approximately 45 minutes.

About 20 minutes before the soup will be ready, put the whole piece of feta cheese onto a baking tray (sheet). Put the chopped (bell) peppers and red onion on top of the feta and drizzle with the olive oil. Bake in the oven for 15–20 minutes.

When the soup is ready, take it off the heat, pour into a blender and blend to the desired consistency.

To serve, pour the soup into bowls, cut chunks of feta and serve a few pieces in the middle of each bowl of soup.

56

Smørrebrød

OPEN SANDWICHES

Smørrebrød, the traditional open Danish sandwiches on rye bread, are as much an everyday part of Danish living as fresh flowers and glittering silver candlesticks on the dining table.

Having grown up for much of my childhood in England, weekends often meant Danish feasts, and open sandwiches were – and still are – exactly that: a feastly treat.

EACH RECIPE SERVES 4

These sandwiches are the standard daily lunch and sometimes dinner for lots of Danish people – they are found in children's packed lunches, on the tables of workshops and in restaurants alike. The toppings can be anything from leftovers of dinner to cold cuts from the butcher or freshly prepared toppings as shown here. There are many restaurants in Denmark serving only these open sandwiches.

58

Æggemad

EGG, TOMATO AND PRAWN

4 eggs

4 x 1cm (½ inch) thick slices of
   freshly baked rye bread (see
   page 208)

salted butter, to spread

8 little gem lettuce leaves

4 tomatoes, thinly sliced

100g (3½oz) prawns (shrimp) in brine,
   or fresh prawns (shrimp) simmered in
   salty water with dill for 2 minutes

mayonnaise, to top

sea salt

freshly ground black pepper

dill, to garnish

Place the eggs in a saucepan of boiling water and boil for 6 minutes, then drain, rinse under cold water and leave to cool. When cool, peel the eggs and cut into slices.

Spread the slices of rye bread with butter. Wash and dry the lettuce leaves, then place them on top of the bread.

Divide the egg and tomato slices between the lettuce leaves, then top with the prawns (shrimp). Add a dollop of mayonnaise on top, season with salt and pepper and garnish with dill.

Makrelsalatmad

SMOKED MACKEREL WITH TOMATO SAUCE

2 tbsp olive oil

1 small onion, finely chopped

1 tsp tomato purée (paste)

4 small tomatoes, chopped

½ tsp pink Himalayan salt or sea salt

2 smoked mackerel fillets, skins removed

juice of ½ lemon

4 x 1cm (½ inch) thick slices of freshly
    baked rye bread (see page 208)

salted butter, to spread

mayonnaise, to top

sea salt

freshly ground black pepper

chopped parsley or chives, to garnish

In a frying pan (skillet), heat the olive oil, then add the onion and gently fry for a few minutes, then add the tomato purée (paste) and simmer for another minute. Next add the chopped tomatoes and salt and simmer for 15 minutes.

Add the smoked mackerel fillets and lemon juice and simmer for 10 minutes, then remove from the heat and leave to cool.

Spread the slices of rye bread with the butter, top with the mackerel in tomato sauce and then add mayonnaise to your liking. Sprinkle with salt and pepper to taste, and garnish with parsley or chives.

Kartoffelmad

NEW POTATO AND CHIVE

12 small new potatoes

1 tsp salt

4 x 1cm (½ inch) thick slices of
    freshly baked rye bread (see
    page 208)

salted butter, to spread

mayonnaise, to top

freshly chopped chives, to garnish

sea salt

freshly ground black pepper

Place the potatoes in a small saucepan, sprinkle over the salt and cover with cold water. Cook over a low heat for exactly 20 minutes, then drain and leave to cool. Spread the slices of rye bread with salted butter.

Once cool, very carefully peel the skin off the potatoes. Cut the potatoes into thin slices and place on top of the buttered rye bread. Top with mayonnaise and lots of chives, a sprinkle of sea salt and black pepper, and devour.

Previous pages, from left to right:
Æggemad, Makrelsalat Mad, Kartoffel Mad.

Tre Slags Sild

THREE TYPES OF HERRING

This classic Danish dish is in fact a selection of probably the most popular and widely consumed fish of the Nordic region. I detested herring growing up, the sight of them and particularly the smell. Age, however, has taken revenge, and the many different kinds of herring, or roll mops as they are referred to in England, have now become a favourite of mine. I particularly love them at Christmas, a time when the Danes truly enjoy Christmas lunches (starting at 6pm) with Danish open sandwiches, beer and schnapps in large quantities.

There are dozens of different types of herrings and marinades. To make them from scratch is a long and very complicated process, therefore I suggest you buy the ready to use plain roll mops. I really like these three, and they are eaten as the first course of open sandwiches, followed by the warm toppings on open sandwiches, and then cheese and dessert.

EACH RECIPE SERVES 4

Kryddersild

SPICED HERRING

8 large plain roll mops, rinsed well

FOR THE SPICED MARINADE

30–40g (1¼–1½oz/⅛ cup) salt

80g (3oz/generous ⅓ cup) sugar

150ml (5fl oz/⅔ cup) red wine vinegar

50ml (2fl oz/scant ¼ cup) water

½ small carrot, thinly sliced

1 small red onion, thinly sliced

1 tsp allspice

2 bay leaves

2 star anise

1 tsp fennel seeds

4 cherry tomatoes, finely chopped

½ tsp raw liquorice powder

TO SERVE

½ red onion, thinly sliced

Place all the spiced marinade ingredients into a saucepan and bring to the boil. Leave to simmer for 10 minutes, then remove from the heat and leave to cool completely.

Cut the roll mops into 2–3cm (¾–1¼ inch) pieces. Add the roll mops to the cold marinade and top with the red onion slices.

Previous pages, from left to right: Marinerede Sild (in bowl), Karrysild (on plate), Kryddersild (in bowl).

Marinerede Sild
CLASSIC MARINATED HERRING

8 large plain roll mops, rinsed well

FOR THE TRADITIONAL MARINADE
160ml (5½fl oz/⅔ cup) white wine
 vinegar or apple cider vinegar
80g (3oz/generous ⅓ cup) raw cane sugar
1 red onion, thinly sliced
10 whole black peppercorns
10 whole red peppercorns
50ml (2fl oz/scant ¼ cup) water
1 carrot, sliced into 20 thin rounds
8 cloves

TO TOP
½ red onion, thinly sliced
dill, to garnish

Place all the marinade ingredients except the cloves in a large saucepan and bring to the boil. Leave to simmer for 5 minutes, then add the cloves, remove from the heat and leave until completely cold.

Cut the roll mops into 2–3cm (¾–1¼ inch) pieces, and when the marinade is cold, pour it over the roll mops.

Transfer the roll mops and marinade into a bowl and add the onion slices and dill to garnish.

The roll mops will keep in a glass jar in the fridge for a couple of weeks.

Karrysild
CURRIED HERRING

8 large plain roll mops, rinsed well
2 eggs (optional)

FOR THE CURRY SAUCE
½ small apple
6 tbsp mayonnaise
2 tbsp crème fraîche
2 tbsp lemon juice
1 tbsp mild curry powder
½ red onion, finely chopped
1 tbsp apricot jam
½ tsp salt
freshly ground black pepper

TO SERVE
buttered rye bread (see page 208)
½ red onion, thinly sliced
capers and chopped chives, to garnish

Slice the roll mops into 2–3cm (¾–1¼ inch) pieces.

Peel, core and finely chop the apple (the tinier the better) for the curry sauce. Mix together all the curry sauce ingredients, then pour it over the roll mops.

If using, place the eggs in a saucepan of cold water, then bring to the boil and boil for 10 minutes. Leave to cool, peel, then chop roughly and add to the curried roll mops.

Spread freshly baked rye bread with salted butter, add the slices of onion and the roll mops and garnish with chives.

TIP
— Put your boiled eggs into cold water as soon as they have had the time you like them cooked for. This prevents the yolk from going brown.

Leverpostej og Dyrlægens Natmad

LIVER PÂTÉ OPEN SANDWICH
AND THE VET'S MIDNIGHT FOOD

MAKES 1 LIVER PÂTÉ

FOR THE LIVER PÂTÉ
70g (2½oz/⅓ cup/scant ¾ stick)
   salted butter
2 tbsp plain (all-purpose) flour
100ml (3½fl oz/scant ½ cup)
   chicken stock
300ml (10fl oz/1¼ cups) single (light)
   cream
400g (14oz) calf's liver
16 rashers (slices) of smoked streaky
   bacon, chopped roughly
1 onion, chopped
4 anchovy fillets
1 egg
2 tbsp fino sherry
pinch of ground allspice
pinch of ground cloves
1 tsp pink Himalayan salt or sea salt

TO SERVE
rye bread (see page 208)
butter, to spread
cucumber slices (optional)
pickled beetroot slices (optional)

FOR THE VET'S MIDNIGHT FOOD
rye bread (see page 208)
butter, to spread
slices of salted or smoked meat
onion slices (optional)
herbs, to garnish (optional)

Liver pâté is without a doubt one of the most popular toppings for an open Danish sandwich. In a country of the packed lunch and open sandwich culture, liver pâté fills most children's lunch boxes on a daily basis. Children tend to prefer liver pâté served very simply on its own, or with pickled beetroot or raw cucumber slices on top, but you can also serve it with fried onions or mushrooms.

A great grown-up version is the vet's midnight food, which is an open sandwich with a thick layer of liver pâté and a slice of salted or smoked meat on top.

Preheat the oven to 180°C/350°F/gas mark 4.

Melt the butter in a saucepan, then add the flour. Stir together and cook for a couple of minutes, then turn the heat down to low and slowly add the stock and then the cream. Cook over a low heat until the mixture reaches a gentle boil, then turn off the heat.

Put the liver, bacon, onion, anchovy fillets, egg and warm cream mixture into a blender or food processor and blend well. You can coarsely blend it, but my children and I prefer it with no lumps.

Pour this mix into a large bowl and add the sherry, allspice, cloves and salt. Pour into a medium-sized loaf tin (pan).

Bake the liver pâté in the oven for 45 minutes. Take out of the oven, and turn the temperature up to 250°C/480°F/gas mark 9. Put the liver pâté back into the hot oven and bake for another 10 minutes to brown the top. Leave to cool.

Butter a slice of rye bread and spread with a thick layer of liver pâté. Add slices of cucumber and pickled beetroot if you wish. Or for the vet's midnight food top with slices of salted or smoked meat, such as smoked pheasant (see page 31), as well as slices of onion and herbs, if you wish.

Pulled Pork med 'Slaw' og Cornichoner

SLOW-COOKED PULLED PORK
AND COLESLAW WITH CORNICHONS

SERVES 6

FOR THE PULLED PORK

2–3kg (4½–6½lb) pork shoulder
2 tbsp sea salt
4 large cloves of garlic, thinly sliced
100ml (3½fl oz/scant ½ cup) olive oil
1 tbsp Dijon mustard
1 tbsp honey
100ml (3½fl oz/scant ½ cup) apple
    cider vinegar

FOR THE SLAW

½ small red cabbage, very thinly sliced
½ small white cabbage, very thinly sliced
½ stick of celery, finely chopped
2 carrots, cut into very thin julienne
8 cornichons, very thinly sliced
6 tbsp mayonnaise
1 tbsp apple cider vinegar
1 tsp mustard
1 tsp honey
1 tbsp white wine vinegar
1 tsp pink Himalayan salt or sea salt

TO SERVE

6 burger buns
pink Himalayan salt or sea salt and
    freshly ground pepper

A long time ago, my flight from Denmark to London was delayed. I had just finished three days of intensive filming and was tired, longing to go home to my kids, and starving! My eyes fell upon a very crunchy looking dark brown baguette filled with meat that looked like shredded duck – another favourite of mine. I ordered the sandwich and learned it was pulled pork. The following day I went straight to the butcher, purchased a pork shoulder and started experimenting. The result is delicious, whether in a bun or as a topping for an open sandwich, and you can cook duck or turkey the same way, which is also incredible.

Preheat the oven to 250°C/480°F/gas mark 9.

Place the pork in a roasting tin (pan). Make 1cm-long (½ inch-long) incisions all over the pork shoulder, then fill the holes with sea salt and garlic. Mix together the olive oil, mustard, honey and apple cider vinegar and smooth it over the pork shoulder.

Roast the pork in the oven for 30 minutes, then take it out and turn the oven temperature down to 180°C/350°F/gas mark 4. Wrap the pork in foil, place in a lidded casserole dish, and put it back into the oven to cook for 6 hours, opening the foil occasionally and spooning the cooking juices over the meat.

While the pork is cooking, prepare the slaw. Put all the chopped vegetables in a large mixing bowl. Mix the rest of the slaw ingredients together in a screwtop jar, shake well, then pour it over the slaw. Massage well with your hands so all the ingredients are mixed together.

Once cooked, shred the pork with a fork. To serve, put a spoonful of the shredded pork onto the bottom half of the burger bun and add a dollop of slaw on the top. Season with salt and pepper, top with the other half of the bun and tuck in.

Chapter Three

Salads

Salat med Røget Makrel og Rugbrødscroutoner

SMOKED MACKEREL SALAD WITH RYE BREAD CROUTONS

SERVES 2

I love to feel the ingredients between my fingers when cooking, so when making my salads I mix the ingredients and dressing together using clean hands.

FOR THE SALAD
small bag of baby spinach leaves,
    about 100g (4oz/3⅓ cups)
2 smoked mackerel fillets
1 avocado
8 small tomatoes on the vine
8 pitted green and black olives
¼ red onion
⅓ cucumber
2 tbsp olive oil
2 tbsp apple cider vinegar
sea salt and freshly ground black pepper
dried red chillies (optional)

FOR THE CROUTONS
2 thick slices of rye bread (see page 208)
4 tbsp olive oil

First make the croutons. Cut the rye bread into squares. Heat the olive oil in a frying pan (skillet) over a medium heat and add the bread squares. Fry for a few minutes on each side until they are golden and crispy, then drain on kitchen towel.

Place the spinach leaves in a large bowl. Tear the mackerel fillets into small pieces, peel, de-stone and cut the avocado into dice, and the tomatoes into chunks, and add to the bowl. Slice the olives and finely chop the onion, then add to the rest of the salad. Finally, skin the cucumber, cut it in half and thinly slice it, then add to the salad bowl.

Shake the olive oil and apple cider vinegar together in a screwtop jar and drizzle over the salad, add the croutons, then mix well.

Season with sea salt, pepper and dried red chillies if you like. Enjoy straight away.

Caesar Salat med Laks

SALMON CAESAR SALAD

SERVES 6–8

FOR THE SALAD

4 large romaine lettuces,
  chopped into thick slices

1 cucumber, skin off, deseeded (if
  you wish), and very thinly sliced

2 avocados, thinly sliced

20 small Niçoise olives

20 baby pickled onions

FOR THE SALMON

6–8 thick fillets of salmon
  (3–4cm/1¼–1½ inches thick),
  skin left on

drizzle of olive oil

juice of 1 lemon

1 tsp pink Himalayan salt or sea salt

FOR THE CROUTONS

100ml (3½fl oz/scant ½ cup) olive oil

2 cloves of garlic, crushed

4 thick slices of rye bread (see page 208)
  or brown baguette, cut into small
  chunks

FOR THE DRESSING

2–4 anchovy fillets (I use 4)

2 tbsp Dijon mustard

1 large clove of garlic

200g (7oz/2 cups) freshly grated
  Parmesan cheese

100ml (3½fl oz/scant ½ cup) olive oil

20ml (¾fl oz/4 tsp) water

2 tbsp lemon juice

Caesar salad will always be on my top ten all-time favourite salads list – and when made with a piece of salmon on top, it's just beyond delicious. This salad is great for lunch or dinner, perfect for a yummy picnic somewhere glorious, and both children and adults alike adore it.

I love this for lunch when I'm in the sun, and also often make it when I'm having dinner alone because it is so easy to make. Sometimes I use fresh lemon juice, olive oil and pink salt instead of the Caesar dressing.

Preheat the oven to 220°C/425°F/gas mark 7. Mix all the salad ingredients together in a large salad bowl.

Place the salmon in an ovenproof dish, drizzle with the olive oil and lemon juice and sprinkle over the salt. Bake in the oven for 15 minutes, then allow to cool. Cut into large chunks.

To make the croutons, heat the oil in a frying pan (skillet) and gently fry the garlic, then add the bread chunks and fry over a low heat for about 5 minutes. Drain on kitchen towel – they will become super crispy as they cool.

To make the dressing, place all the dressing ingredients in a blender or food processor and blend until smooth. Pour the dressing over the salad and mix in well with your hands so all the salad is coated.

Serve the salad with the salmon and croutons carefully mixed in.

NOTE

– Many people today enjoy semi-cooked salmon. For this, bake the salmon in the oven for 12 minutes (rather than 15 minutes as above); if you prefer it well done, then bake for up to 25 minutes.

Hvid Asparges med Rejer

WHITE ASPARAGUS AND PRAWN SALAD

SERVES 4–6

FOR THE SALAD

16–20 white asparagus spears

1 tsp salt

4 tbsp olive oil

1 small red onion, finely chopped

1 small clove of garlic, finely chopped
(optional)

250g (9oz) uncooked prawns (shrimp)

8 cherry tomatoes, finely chopped

1 avocado, cut into small cubes

½ cucumber, skinned, deseeded and
cut into small cubes

400g (14oz/13 cups) spinach leaves
or romaine lettuce leaves, roughly
chopped

FOR THE DRESSING

juice of ½ lemon

½ tsp pink Himalayan salt or sea salt

100ml (3½fl oz/scant ½ cup) olive oil

2 tbsp asparagus water (reserved from
cooking the asparagus)

Is there anything more delicious than white asparagus when in season? Served with homemade Hollandaise sauce or a simple vinaigrette, this is a salad I started making when I began working as a model. I needed healthy food that was easy to make, tasted delicious, and was suitable for any time of day or night. All my salads are pretty simple and very scrummy I think, so enjoy.

First prepare the asparagus. Hold the tip of the asparagus head and try to bend it two-thirds of the way down the stalk – the asparagus should break off where the tender stalk ends. Otherwise trim the bottom 3cm (1¼ inches) of the asparagus and peel the stem with a vegetable peeler.

Bring a saucepan of water to the boil, add the salt, then add the asparagus and simmer for 2–4 minutes. Drain (reserving 2 tbsp of the cooking water) and leave the asparagus to cool, then cut into 3cm (1¼ inch) pieces.

Place all the ingredients for the dressing in a screwtop jar and shake to combine. Set aside until needed.

In a frying pan (skillet), heat the olive oil and add the onion and garlic. Fry for a couple of minutes, then add the prawns and fry for a couple more minutes until cooked through. Take off the heat.

To make the salad, place the asparagus pieces and prawns in a large bowl, add the chopped tomatoes, avocado, cucumber and spinach leaves. Pour over the dressing and mix well using your hands so the ingredients really come together. Serve straight away.

NOTE

– Nowadays most things can be eaten raw, and I love eating raw asparagus. Simply cut the asparagus into very thin slices, always discarding the bottom 3cm (1¼ inch) or so of the asparagus stalk.

Hummerhalesalat

LOBSTER TAIL SALAD

SERVES 8

FOR THE LOBSTER TAILS

2 tbsp raw cane sugar (optional)

1 tbsp pink Himalayan salt or sea salt

1 slice of lemon

4 stalks of dill

400g (14oz) lobster tails, crayfish tails
   or large prawns (shrimp)

FOR THE SALAD

100g (3½oz/scant ½ cup) mayonnaise

100g (3½oz/scant ½ cup) crème fraîche

2 tbsp lemon juice or apple cider
   vinegar

30g (1¼oz/⅔ cup) dill, finely chopped,
   plus extra to garnish

20g (¾oz/scant ½ cup) chives, finely
   chopped, plus extra to garnish

Tabasco or chilli paste, to taste (optional)

pink Himalayan salt or sea salt, to taste

freshly ground black pepper, to taste

8 crispy cos salad leaves

TO SERVE

8 slices of rye bread (see page 208)

butter, to spread

dill and chives, to garnish

This salad is adored in my family, and is a lovely starter or summer lunch. Its origins are in Sweden, and my Swedish mother and grandmother were both experts at making this. You can use lobster tails, crayfish tails or large prawns (shrimp), depending on what is available. Fresh dill is a herb that complements most fish and crustaceans. In Scandinavia, we even add fresh dill when boiling new potatoes.

Bring a saucepan of water to the boil. Add the sugar, salt, lemon and dill, then add the lobster tails and simmer for 5 minutes, then drain.

Mix together the mayonnaise, crème fraîche, lemon juice (or vinegar) and finely chopped herbs. Season to taste with the Tabasco, salt and pepper.

Add the cooked lobster tails to the mayonnaise mix and stir well to combine.

Lay out the cos salad leaves on a serving plate, then divide the lobster and mayonnaise mix equally between the salad leaves. Sprinkle with extra chopped dill and chives if you wish.

Toast and butter the rye bread, then serve alongside the salad. Perfect on a summer's day.

Min Fars Kyllingesalat

MY FATHER'S DELICIOUS CHICKEN SALAD

SERVES 4

FOR THE SALAD
400g (14oz) roast chicken leftovers
    or grilled (broiled) chicken breast,
    cooled
200g (7oz) celeriac (celery root)
4 sticks of celery

FOR THE DRESSING
4 tbsp mayonnaise
4 tbsp crème fraîche
1 tsp Dijon mustard
1 tsp curry powder
½ tsp pink Himalayan salt or sea salt
1 tbsp olive oil
1 tbsp lemon juice
¼ tsp raw cane sugar

TO SERVE
thick slices of rye bread (see page 208),
    toasted
chives, finely chopped, to garnish

My father was always very creative about using leftovers from various meat cuts including roast chicken. If we had a dish with bones, these would never be discarded before a fabulous stock had been made using the bones from meat, fish or poultry alike. My father even had a freezer in his house exclusively for his homemade stocks.

This dish is a family favourite, and I think we are almost more excited about this dish than the actual roast chicken the day before. This salad is delicious served with toasted rye bread or as a light bite in a little gem lettuce leaf.

Chop the chicken, celeriac (celery root) and celery into small dice, then place in a large mixing bowl and mix together.

Mix all the dressing ingredients together until smooth, then pour over the salad. Mix together well with your hands.

Serve the salad on the rye bread, with chopped chives scattered on top.

Lun Hovedsalat med Bacon, Valnødder og Blåskimmelost

WARM LITTLE GEM SALAD WITH BACON,
WALNUTS AND DANISH BLUE CHEESE DRESSING

SERVES 4

FOR THE SALAD
1 tbsp olive oil
16 whole walnuts, halved
8 rashers (slices) of streaky bacon
2 tbsp salt
4 little gem lettuces, cut in half

FOR THE DRESSING
200g (7oz) Danish blue cheese,
   roughly chopped
6 tbsp olive oil
3 tbsp white wine vinegar or lemon juice
½ tsp Dijon mustard
2 tbsp water

TO SERVE
fresh herbs, to garnish

This dish is one I first came across as a child in St Croix, in the US Virgin Islands, a Danish colony until it was sold to the Americans in 1916. I have also enjoyed it while travelling in America, visiting my sister when she studied History of Art at UVA (University of Virginia). Most often served raw, rather than blanched, I have always wondered if the Americans were perhaps inspired by the Danes? Either way, it's a classic and utterly delicious salad. When blanched, I love how the cheese melts into the crunchy yet soft salad leaves; when raw, the different textures are also wonderful together, more refreshing and summery than the warm wintry blanched salad.

To make the dressing, mix all the ingredients together in a screwtop jar, shake carefully and set aside.

Heat the olive oil in a frying pan (skillet) and gently fry the walnuts for a couple of minutes, then place on kitchen towel to dry. Fry the bacon in the same pan until crispy, then place on kitchen towel to dry. Roughly chop the bacon and walnuts.

Bring a saucepan of water to the boil and add the salt. Gently lower the halved lettuces into the water using a slotted spoon. Leave for 1 minute. Carefully take out and drain well on kitchen towel or a clean tea towel, making sure all the excess water has drained off.

Divide the lettuce leaves carefully between 4 plates so the leaves don't separate, then scatter over the bacon and walnuts.

Drizzle the dressing over the top of the salad, scatter over fresh herbs if you wish, and serve immediately.

Vilde Svampe Salat

WILD MUSHROOM SALAD

SERVES 4–6

700g (1lb 9oz) of 3 different kinds of
   mushroom: safely foraged wild
   mushrooms or I used 300g (10½oz)
   chestnut, 300g (10½oz) button
   and 100g (3½oz) chanterelle
   mushrooms

2 tbsp sesame seeds, white or mixed

4–6 tbsp olive oil

2 tbsp lemon juice

2 tbsp apple cider vinegar

½ tsp pink Himalayan salt or sea salt

4 tbsp finely chopped parsley, plus
   extra to garnish

1 small clove of garlic, finely chopped

6 small vine tomatoes, finely chopped

1 small avocado, cut into cubes

½ red onion, finely chopped

⅔ heart of palm, finely chopped
   (optional)

2 grilled (broiled) artichokes, finely
   chopped (optional)

Mushrooms remind me so much of my childhood. My mother was an amazing expert at recognizing all the different varieties, edible or not, when we spent many an hour out in the woods picking them. It was always the most cosy time spent as a family, and very Scandinavian – being outdoors as a family, collecting and then preparing feasts to enjoy. Mushrooms and blueberries are, for me, symbols of complete and utter joy, uniting us humans with mother nature.

Prepare the mushrooms – clean, then cut any large mushrooms into quarters, leaving the smaller chanterelles whole.

Heat a frying pan (skillet) over a medium heat and add the sesame seeds. Lightly toast them in the pan – use a lid as they do pop and jump around – then set aside.

Mix the mushrooms with the olive oil, lemon juice, apple cider vinegar and salt. Leave to marinate for 5 minutes.

Add the parsley and garlic to the mushrooms and mix well. Add the remaining ingredients and lastly the toasted sesame seeds. Mix a final time, garnish with a little extra parsley and serve straight away.

This salad is also delicious with a slice of nut bread (see page 209) toasted in a little olive oil.

Sprød Gulerodssalat med Ristet Kerner

CRUNCHY CARROT SALAD WITH TOASTED SEEDS

SERVES 2 AS A MAIN COURSE
OR 6 AS A SIDE DISH

FOR THE CARROT SALAD

12 large, sweet, crunchy carrots

6 tbsp pumpkin seeds

6 tbsp sunflower seeds

2 tbsp linseeds (flaxseeds)

2 tbsp hemp seeds

2 tbsp sesame seeds

FOR THE DRESSING

10 tbsp olive oil

4 tbsp soy sauce

3 tbsp sweet and sticky balsamic vinegar

½ tsp pink Himalayan salt or sea salt

In my modelling days, one of the things I loved most about coming home from my travels around the world was my kitchen, and having the time to cook. For as long as I can remember, I have found food preparation therapeutic and relaxing, a treat in fact, one of life's greatest luxuries. It is my greatest passion and my favourite hobby.

I adore cooking more than anything, and find it so rewarding to experiment with our planet's incredible ingredients. This salad has travelled with me across the continents – simple to make and to source because carrots are grown everywhere, and seeds are easy to pack in a small suitcase.

This salad can be used as a side dish to any fish, chicken or meat main course, or on its own for a light but fulfilling meal. I often make a ginormous portion and have it as a main course on my own in front of a good movie – it's so delicious, comforting and fabulous, yet at the same time super-healthy and filling as seeds are such a great source of protein and good fatty oils. It is also delicious the day after you make it, only a little less crunchy, which I quite like.

Peel the carrots, then cut into long, thin slices and then into thin strips. Put the carrot juliennes in a large salad bowl.

Heat a large frying pan (skillet), then add all the seeds for the salad and toast until golden, moving them around in the pan so they do not burn. Pour most of the seeds over the carrots.

Put all the dressing ingredients into a screwtop jar and shake well. Pour the dressing over the salad and mix well using your hands, then scatter the rest of the seeds over the top. So simple, but so delicious!

Kikærtesalat med Oliven, Rødløg og Tomater

CHICKPEA SALAD WITH OLIVES, RED ONION AND TOMATOES

SERVES 6–8

FOR THE CHICKPEAS

200g (7oz/1 cup) dried chickpeas
  (garbanzo beans)
1 tsp salt

FOR THE SALAD

12 cherry tomatoes
16 pitted black olives, sliced
1 avocado, cubed
1 small red onion, finely chopped
100g (3½oz) Jerusalem artichokes,
  chopped
1 long red Romano pepper, finely chopped
1 stick of celery, cubed
1 tbsp chopped coriander (cilantro)
1 tbsp chopped basil
100g (3½oz/⅔ cup) roasted pine nuts

FOR THE DRESSING

8 tbsp olive oil
3 tbsp apple cider vinegar
½ tsp pink Himalayan salt
  or sea salt
½ tsp dried chilli and garlic flakes

TO GARNISH
fresh herbs

Simple yet delicious, perfect for breakfast, lunch or dinner, this salad is packed full of goodness and delicious flavours. It's also great for eating the next day as the flavours strengthen well, so is an ideal dish to make a double portion of the night before and take to work for lunch, or to enjoy on a summer picnic.

Place the chickpeas (garbanzo beans) in a large bowl. Cover with water, so the water is at least 2cm (¾ inch) above the chickpeas (garbanzo beans) and leave overnight.

Drain the chickpeas (garbanzo beans), then place in a saucepan with the salt and cover with water. Bring to the boil, then gently simmer for 45 minutes. Drain and leave to cool.

Mix all the dressing ingredients together in the bottom of a large salad bowl. Now add all the salad ingredients and chickpeas (garbanzo beans) and mix well with your hands so all the ingredients absorb the dressing nicely.

Enjoy this yummy salad straight away, garnished with fresh herbs, or store in the fridge and enjoy later or the next day.

NOTE

– I always use dried chickpeas (garbanzo beans), but if you don't have time you can skip the first 2 steps and use 2 x 400g (14oz) cans of chickpeas (garbanzo beans).

Chapter Four

Main Courses:
Meat

Fines Frikadeller

FINE'S MEATBALLS WITH SPICED RED CABBAGE

SERVES 6

FOR THE MEATBALLS

1 small onion, finely grated

500g (1lb 2oz) minced (ground) turkey,
    pork or veal

1 egg

2 tbsp oats

100ml (3½fl oz/scant ½ cup) milk

½ tsp pink Himalayan salt or sea salt

FOR FRYING THE MEATBALLS

1 tbsp butter

2 tbsp olive oil

FOR THE RED CABBAGE

2 tbsp duck (or goose) fat (see page 142)

1 red cabbage, quartered then thinly
    sliced

1 small Cox's apple, peeled, cored
    and grated

300ml (10fl oz/1¼ cups) bone broth,
    chicken stock or water

50ml (2fl oz/scant ¼ cup) apple cider
    vinegar

300ml (10fl oz/1¼ cups) red wine

1 bay leaf

1 cinnamon stick

1 tbsp raw cane sugar

2 tsp pink Himalayan salt or sea salt

TO SERVE

mustard

parsley, roughly chopped

Every year when we went skiing as kids, we would drive to the Alps. Mummy's cold meatballs and buttered rye bread would be our lunch during the long drive – that lovely taste still lingers.

There are probably as many variations of meatballs in Denmark as there are families! I grew up with many different types of meatballs: my mother's often resembled small truffles when she made Swedish meatballs, or large plums when she made Danish ones; my grandmother's were like a new potato; and my children's favourite (and mine) are many and vary in size and flavour, depending on whether I use veal, pork, beef, turkey or chicken. These meatballs are a favourite of my daughter, Josephine, and are a good marriage of all the ones we in my little family love.

The red cabbage goes perfectly with the meatballs, and can also be used on open sandwiches, for example with *leverpostej* (liver pâté, see page 64) or *flæskesteg* (roast pork, see page 112).

Mix all the meatball ingredients together in a large bowl. Once combined, knead with your hands to form a ball, then leave in the fridge for an hour for the flavours to develop.

Make the spiced red cabbage. Melt the duck fat in a large lidded saucepan, then add the red cabbage and apple and sauté for a minute. Then add the broth, apple cider vinegar, red wine, bay leaf, cinnamon stick, sugar and salt. Put on the lid and simmer for 10 minutes, then remove the lid and simmer for 50 minutes over a low heat, stirring regularly so that it does not stick to the pan.

After the meatball mix has rested, form the meatballs to the shape and size you like. Melt the butter in a frying pan (skillet) and add the oil. Fry the meatballs for about 5 minutes on each side until they are crispy and golden (timings will vary depending on size).

Serve the meatballs and cabbage hot with mustard and a sprinkling of chopped parsley. I love these with buttered rye bread or boiled and peeled new potatoes.

Krebinetter med Urtedressing

PORK PATTIES WITH HERB DRESSING
AND CRUNCHY ELEVEN-VEGETABLE SALAD

SERVES 6

FOR THE *KREBINETTER*
600g (1lb 5oz) minced (ground) pork
½ tsp pink Himalayan salt or sea salt
2 eggs
8 tbsp breadcrumbs
1 tbsp chopped chives
1 small carrot, grated
1 small courgette (zucchini), grated
25g (1oz/2 tbsp) butter

FOR THE HERB DRESSING
250ml (8½fl oz/1 cup) sour cream
   or crème fraîche
1 clove of garlic, crushed
½ tsp pink Himalayan salt or sea salt
1 tbsp finely chopped parsley
1 tbsp finely chopped basil
1 tbsp finely chopped coriander (cilantro)
1 tbsp finely chopped tarragon
2 tbsp lemon juice

I remember falling in love with this dish years ago at my old boarding school, Herlufsholm Kostskole – *krebinetter* was in fact the hot meal that I enjoyed the most there. At school it was served with a pasta salad, which I found too soft. What I really love here is the warm and soft patties meeting the crunchy and salty salad – my idea of a fantastic combo.

Remember ingredients can always, in my opinion, be exchanged for something else. Don't let not having a few ingredients hold you back – improvise! We are all 'perfectly imperfect', which is what I love so much about humanity.

First make the herb dressing. Mix all the ingredients together in a screwtop jar, shake well, and place in the fridge for at least 30 minutes before serving.

Prepare the salad, seeds and salad dressing (see opposite).

To make the krebinetter, put all the ingredients except the butter into a blender or food processor and blend until well mixed and combined. Remove the meat from the blender, divide into 12 balls, and shape each one into a patty or burger shape.

Melt the butter in a large frying pan (skillet) over a medium heat. Fry the krebinetter for around 5 minutes on each side until browned and cooked through.

Serve the krebinetter with the dressed salad on the side and the herb dressing in a separate dish so people can help themselves.

FOR THE CRUNCHY ELEVEN-
VEGETABLE SALAD

2 carrots, cut into long, thin strips

1 long red Romano pepper,
  cut into thin strips

½ small red cabbage, cut into thin slices

½ small white cabbage, cut into thin
  slices

100g (3½oz/1½ cups) chopped kale
  leaves (stalks discarded)

½ cucumber, skin removed, cut into
  thin strips

3 spring onions (scallions), cut into
  thin strips

100g (3½oz/3⅓ cups) baby spinach,
  cut into thin strips

1 courgette (zucchini), cut into thin strips

1 avocado, thinly sliced

½ red onion, cut into strips

FOR THE SEEDS

2 tbsp sesame seeds

2 tbsp sunflower seeds

2 tbsp pumpkin seeds

2 tbsp hemp seeds

FOR THE SALAD DRESSING

6–8 tbsp olive oil

3 tbsp soy sauce

2 tbsp balsamic vinegar

¼ tsp mustard powder

1 tbsp chopped coriander (cilantro)

¼ tsp salt

To make the salad, mix all the salad ingredients together in an enormous salad bowl.

Heat a frying pan (skillet) until hot, then add the 4 kinds of seeds. Toast them in the pan, moving them about so they become golden, then remove from the pan.

To make the dressing, mix all the dressing ingredients together in a screwtop jar and shake well.

When ready to serve, scatter the seeds over the salad, pour the dressing over the top and massage well into the salad ingredients using your hands.

Boller i Karry

PORK MEATBALLS IN CURRY SAUCE

SERVES 6

It doesn't really get much more Danish than this. The Danes introduce this dish as soon as solids are given to their children, with or without the curry sauce. Funnily enough, it has taken me years to really appreciate this gorgeous and very cosy dish of meatballs in curry, but it is now one that I enjoy immensely each time I have it. It's as *hyggeligt* as it gets…

FOR THE MEATBALLS

600g (1lb 5oz) minced (ground) pork

1 yellow onion, thinly sliced

2 eggs

2 tbsp breadcrumbs

1 tbsp cornflour (cornstarch) or
  potato flour

100ml (3½fl oz/scant ½ cup) milk

½ tsp salt

To make the meatballs, put all the ingredients for the meatballs into a blender or food processor and blend well. Remove from the blender and shape into balls the size of golf balls.

FOR COOKING THE MEATBALLS

600ml (1 pint/2½ cups) vegetable
  or chicken stock

In a large saucepan, heat the stock until simmering, then add the meatballs and cook for 10–15 minutes. Once cooked, remove the meatballs with a slotted spoon. Sieve the stock into a measuring jug and reserve the stock for the sauce.

FOR THE CURRY SAUCE

2 tbsp butter

1 red onion, finely chopped

1 small apple, peeled and cored,
  cut into small dice

1 small banana, cut into small dice

1 tbsp plain (all-purpose) flour

1 tbsp curry powder

½ tsp ground cinnamon

½ tsp pink Himalayan salt or sea salt

400ml (13½fl oz/1⅔ cups) coconut
  milk

400ml (13½fl oz/1⅔ cups) liquid reserved
  from cooking the meatballs

To make the curry sauce, melt the butter in a saucepan over a medium–low heat, add the red onion and gently fry for a couple of minutes. Add the apple and banana and cook, stirring. Sieve in the flour and add the curry powder, cinnamon and salt, mixing well. Now turn down the heat to low and slowly add the coconut milk, stirring as you add it.

Add the reserved meatball stock and allow the sauce to simmer for 15 minutes. Take off the heat and blend in a blender or food processor. Pour back into the saucepan and if necessary add more of the meatball stock until the sauce has the consistency of a good soup. Now add the meatballs to the sauce and warm through thoroughly over a low heat.

TO SERVE

450g (1lb/2⅓ cups) long-grain rice

Meanwhile, cook the rice according to the packet instructions.

Serve the hot meatballs with the rice.

Stegt Flæsk med Persillesovs

CRISPY FRIED PORK SLICES WITH PARSLEY SAUCE

SERVES 4

FOR THE PORK
600g (1lb 5oz) pork belly, or thick
    smoked bacon
sprinkle of pink Himalayan salt or
    sea salt

FOR THE POTATOES
600g (1lb 5oz) baby new potatoes
1 tsp salt

FOR THE PARSLEY SAUCE
30g (1¼oz/2 tbsp) butter
3 tbsp plain (all-purpose) flour
400ml (13½fl oz/1⅔ cups) milk
100ml (3½fl oz/scant ½ cup) water
    from the boiled potatoes
80g (3oz/1¼ cups) finely chopped
    parsley
sea salt and freshly ground black
    pepper, to season

TO GARNISH
chives
parsley

This dish was officially named Denmark's national dish in 2014. It is an incredible dish in so many ways – it's no wonder that it's hard to stop eating it once you start. We didn't consume it too often growing up because it is so very filling and rich, and we would always overeat when it was made.

There was a special restaurant called Fabrikken where I used to enjoy this as a teenager. Now it is a dish that I crave maybe twice a year, and if I go to a restaurant that serves it, I order it without a shadow of a doubt. It's worth making more of this dish than you expect people to eat, as this is one dish where you just can't stop.

Cut the pork belly into 5mm (¼ inch) thin slices and sprinkle with salt, then leave for a couple of hours before cooking.

When ready to cook, preheat the oven to 200°C/400°F/gas mark 6. Put the potatoes in a saucepan with water covering them and add the salt. Bring to the boil, simmer for 20 minutes, then turn them off. They can stand happily in the water for a while until you need some of the water for the parsley sauce. The potatoes can either be served like this or peeled first, which is the way we love them in my family.

Once the potatoes are boiling, put the pork slices onto a large baking tray (sheet) and cook in the oven for about 30 minutes, turning regularly, until the pieces are very crispy. When they are ready, take them out and place them on kitchen towel to dry.

To make the parsley sauce, melt the butter in a saucepan, then add the flour and cook, stirring, for a few minutes. Now, very slowly on a very low heat, gradually add the milk and then the potato water and continue to cook, whisking well so there are no lumps. The sauce should have a lovely smooth consistency. Add the parsley and season with salt and pepper to taste.

Serve the crispy pork, new potatoes sprinkled with chives, and parsley sauce. Garnish with a little extra parsley and enjoy.

Flæskesteg

ROAST PORK WITH CRACKLING

SERVES 6

FOR THE PORK

1.5kg (3lb 5oz) joint of pork,
   suitable for crackling (see right)

2 tbsp coarse sea salt

6 bay leaves

TO SERVE

caramelized potatoes (see page 143)

red cabbage (see page 143)

I have always thought that *flæskesteg* was the Danish national dish, but after having done a little research, I found that, although it was in amongst the contenders, it lost out to its brother, *stegt flaesk* (fried pork slices, see page 108).

This is a dish that many Danish families enjoy on Christmas Eve, but the love of it is so great that any occasion, any day of the year will do. I like to use different parts of the pork for this dish – as long as the skin will crackle well, you can use the loin (with the ribs left in, or removed), leg or shoulder.

Flæskesteg is also a classic topping, cold or warm, in thin slices on open Danish sandwiches with red cabbage, or as in my brother-in-law's case, with buttered rye bread and a layer of mustard.

Preheat the oven to 200°C/400°F/gas mark 6.

Prepare the pork for the crackling, unless you have already asked your butcher to do so. Using a very sharp knife, cut long grooves into the pork rind, about 5mm (¼ inch) deep and about 5mm (¼ inch) apart, being careful not to cut right down to the meat.

Put the pork into a roasting tin (pan) with the crackling facing down. Add just enough boiling water to cover the crackling and roast in the oven for 30 minutes.

Take the pork out of the oven, carefully turn it over so the crackling is now facing upwards, drain the water and massage the salt into the crackling. Put the bay leaves into the incisions in the crackling.

Turn the oven down to 180°C/350°F/gas mark 4, then return the pork to the oven and roast for 1 hour. After 1 hour, turn the heat up to 220°C/425°F/gas mark 7 and roast for another 5 minutes so the crackling becomes super crispy. Rest for 5 minutes before slicing.

Serve the pork with the caramelized potatoes and red cabbage.

Min Mors Lækre Svenske Pølseret

MY MOTHER'S DELICIOUS SWEDISH SAUSAGE CASSEROLE

SERVES 6

FOR THE SAUSAGE CASSEROLE

500g (1lb 2oz) baby potatoes

1 tbsp butter

2 tbsp olive oil

1 red onion, finely chopped

1 tbsp tomato purée (paste)

12 smoked pork sausages (frankfurters),
  thinly sliced

4 tbsp tomato ketchup

½ tsp pink Himalayan salt or sea salt

300ml (10fl oz/1¼ cups) single (light)
  cream

TO SERVE

chives, to garnish

green peas or rye bread (see page 208)

Childhood birthdays, cold winter evenings, weekend lunches, children laughing, candles burning, fires crackling – happy days. It feels like there was never a bad day back then, families prioritized their family, and friends were always a constant stream in and out of the house. Food was prepared all the time, and the icing on the cake came in the various shapes and sizes of good food, prepared lovingly together by the adults while the children played, or with the children helping to cook or lay the table – anything for everyone to be together in the same room, spending quality *hyggelig* time together.

Put the potatoes into a saucepan of cold salted water and bring to the boil. Boil for 20 minutes, drain, leave to cool and then peel off the skins.

In a large saucepan, melt the butter and add the olive oil. Add the onions and fry gently, then add the tomato purée (paste) and fry over a medium heat for a few minutes to 'burn it off'. Add the sausages and cook for 1 minute, then add the ketchup and salt and stir well. Lastly, add the cream and leave to simmer on a very low heat for 10 minutes.

Cut the potatoes into small chunks and add to the sauce. Warm through, then serve, garnished with chives. This is delicious with green peas, or with freshly baked and buttered rye bread.

Gule Ærter

YELLOW PEAS WITH SMOKED SAUSAGE

SERVES 6

FOR THE PEAS AND PORK BELLY
500g (1lb 2oz/2¼ cups) yellow split peas
2.5 litres (4 pints/10 cups) vegetable
    stock or water
1kg (2¼lb) pork belly
2 sprigs of thyme

FOR THE SMOKED SAUSAGE
400g (14oz) thick smoked
    sausages
250g (9oz) chorizo sausages

FOR THE VEGETABLE SOUP
4 tbsp olive oil
4 small red onions, finely chopped
2 carrots, finely chopped
1 stick of celery, finely chopped
1 large leek, thinly sliced
1 sprig of thyme
1.5 litres (2½ pints/6 cups) vegetable
    or chicken stock or water
1 tsp salt

This is the most perfect 'winter pot'. Rich in flavour and consistency, protein and carbs are in ideal quantities.

This dish was often served for shooting lunches or on very cold winter nights. An utterly delicious and classic Danish meal, this is a brilliant choice to have with children and friends alike. It also tastes amazing the next day.

If possible, soak the yellow split peas overnight in a bowl of water.

Preheat the oven to 200°C/400°F/gas mark 6.

Drain the yellow split peas, then place in a saucepan, cover with water and bring to the boil. Boil for 40 minutes if you have soaked them, or 90 minutes if unsoaked, then drain. Transfer the peas to a large saucepan with the vegetable stock, add the pork belly and thyme and simmer for 1 hour, occasionally checking and removing any foam from the top.

When the peas and pork have been simmering for about 40 minutes, in another large saucepan make the soup. Heat the oil, add the vegetables and herbs, fry for a couple of minutes and then pour in the stock. Add the salt, bring to the boil and simmer for 20 minutes.

Once the soup has come to the boil, put the smoked pork and chorizo sausages in a roasting tin (pan) and cook in the oven for about 20 minutes. When browned and cooked, remove from the oven and cut into thick slices.

Once the pork belly is cooked, remove from the saucepan and wrap in foil to keep warm. Remove and discard the thyme sprigs. Drain the yellow peas and mash well.

Mix the vegetable soup and the mashed yellow peas together, then serve in bowls. Thinly slice the pork belly and add a slice of pork and a piece of each kind of sausage to each bowl.

Pariserbøf

PARISIAN STEAK WITH FRIED EGG
AND PICKLED BEETROOT (BEET)

SERVES 6

FOR THE PARISIAN STEAK
900g (2lb) good-quality scraped or
    minced (ground) steak
2 eggs
2 tbsp finely chopped capers
    (I leave these out if I'm making
    this for my children)
1 tsp pink Himalayan salt or sea salt
6 slices of fresh bread
2 tbsp olive oil
1 tbsp butter

FOR THE FRIED ONIONS
1 tbsp butter
1 large red onion, thinly sliced

FOR THE FRIED EGGS
2 tbsp olive oil
6 eggs

TO SERVE
1 whole pickled beetroot (beet),
    cut into small cubes
6 tbsp freshly grated horseradish

In Denmark we have lots of fantastic and very classic restaurants for both lunch and dinner. When the menu is really traditional, *Pariserbøf* will surely be on it. It is full of great succulent flavours and is a dish that is as old-fashioned and traditional as it gets. It is like a 'glamorous' version of a burger.

Preheat the oven to 150°C/300°F/gas mark 2.

Mix the scraped steak meat, eggs, capers (if using) and salt together and shape into 6 large, flat burgers.

Put a burger onto each slice of bread and press down firmly but gently, making sure the burgers don't lose their shape.

Melt the oil and butter together in a large frying pan (skillet) over a medium heat, then fry the meat side of the burger for about 4 minutes or until well cooked. Turn over to the bread side and fry for another 3 minutes until the bread is golden and crispy. Transfer to a baking tray (sheet) and leave in the warm oven while you prepare the rest of the food.

Melt the butter in another frying pan (skillet). Add the red onion and fry until golden and crispy, then transfer to a bowl and place in the warm oven.

Heat the olive oil in the same pan you cooked the onions in, and fry the eggs until cooked to your taste.

Take the Parisian steaks out of the oven and put one on each plate, then top with an egg. Add a little pickled beetroot (beet) and horseradish to the plate. Serve immediately with the crispy fried onion and some salad leaves or my kale and quinoa salad (see page 93) on the side.

Hakkebøf

DANISH HAMBURGERS WITH FRIED ONIONS
AND LENTIL SALAD

SERVES 6

FOR THE *HAKKEBØF*
900g (2lb) minced (ground) beef
2 eggs
2 tbsp oats
½ tsp pink Himalayan salt or sea salt

FOR THE FRIED ONIONS
2 tbsp olive oil
2 tsp butter
2 yellow onions, thinly sliced
1 tsp raw cane sugar

FOR THE LENTIL SALAD
250g (9oz/1¼ cups) green or brown
    lentils
1 tbsp pink Himalayan salt or sea salt,
    plus ½ tsp
12 cherry tomatoes
1 small red onion, finely chopped
2 tbsp chopped parsley
4 tbsp olive oil

TO GARNISH
parsley sprigs

These burgers are true Danish 'sliders'; and I think that this is really a man's dish at heart. But what can I say... I think there's a man in all of us somewhere!

The *hakkebøf* is delicious, classically served with the soft fried onions and lentils. It is also just as good the next day, chopped up and added to a tomato sauce to go with pasta, if you have some leftover burgers.

First make the lentil salad. In a sieve, rinse the lentils well under cold running water. Place in a saucepan and add enough water to cover them completely. Bring to the boil, add 1 tbsp of pink Himalayan salt and a little more water to make sure the lentils are covered, then turn down to a simmer. Simmer for 15 minutes.

Place the tomatoes, onion, parsley, olive oil and ½ tsp pink Himalayan salt in a large bowl and mix well. When the lentils are cooked, drain and add them to the tomato mixture. Leave to cool while you make the burgers.

In a large bowl, mix the beef together with the eggs, oats and salt. Divide the mix into 6 balls and make 6 round burger shapes.

Next cook the fried onions. In a large frying pan (skillet), melt the olive oil and butter over a low heat. Add the onions and sugar and fry for about 10 minutes until soft, then remove the onions from the pan and set aside.

In the same pan, fry the burgers over a medium heat for 4 minutes on each side. Fry in batches if necessary.

Serve the burgers with the onions on top, the lentil salad on the side, and garnish with parsley. This is also delicious with toasted rye bread (see page 208) or new or roasted potatoes.

Biksemad

'A MIX OF EVERYTHING'

SERVES 6

FOR THE *BIKSEMAD*
500g (1lb 2oz) whole cooked potatoes
olive oil, for frying
1 large yellow onion, finely chopped
100g (3½oz) salami, finely diced
600g (1lb 5oz) leftover cooked meat
    (any meat, or a mix of meats, works
    well), cut into chunks
6 eggs

TO SERVE
your choice of sauce: I like
    Worcestershire sauce, Tabasco sauce,
    tomato ketchup and HP sauce

This is a classic and deeply loved Danish everyday dish. It's perfect for when you have any kind of leftover meat to use up, or even a mixture of leftover meats. It's one of my favourite dinners, and one I have enjoyed since I was a child. It is also one of my children's absolute favourite dishes. I am a great believer in trying never to waste anything, and to recycle whenever possible.

I love it served with Worcestershire sauce, Tabasco sauce, tomato ketchup and HP sauce, flavours my father introduced me to.

Cut the potatoes into tiny cubes. Heat the olive oil in a large frying pan (skillet). Add the potatoes and fry until golden and crispy, then remove the potatoes from the pan and set aside.

Add the onions to the frying pan (skillet) and fry until softened and browned, then add the salami and fry for a couple of minutes. Add the cooked meat and potatoes and cook for a couple of minutes to heat through.

Meanwhile, heat a little oil in a separate frying pan (skillet) and fry the eggs.

Serve up 6 portions of *biksemad* and top each with a fried egg. Have a range of sauces so people can add their favourite.

Oksehøjreb med Flødekartofler og Sovs

RIB OF BEEF WITH BAKED CREAMY POTATOES
AND BONE MARROW SAUCE

SERVES 6

FOR THE RIB OF BEEF

2kg (4½lb) rib of beef on the bone

4 tbsp olive oil, to brush

2 tbsp pink Himalayan salt or sea salt

FOR THE BONE MARROW SAUCE

2kg (4½lb) beef or veal bones with
  bone marrow (ask your butcher)

8 large carrots, cut into chunks

2 large onions, quartered

1 whole garlic bulb, cut in half

2 sticks of celery, cut into chunks

20 cherry tomatoes

1 bouquet garni

1 tsp pink Himalayan salt or sea salt

5 litres (10 pints/20 cups) water

300ml (10fl oz/1¼ cups) white
  or red wine

The king of all beef dishes in my opinion – and my father was without a shadow of doubt the master of this dish. When made well, the bone marrow sauce is like a thick syrup in its consistency, and when served with the beef and creamy potatoes it's just heaven on a plate. It's a real treat, a very special meal, so devour every mouthful to your heart's content – and always remember to chew well. It is much easier for the body to digest well-chewed food, so the more you chew, the more your body benefits from all the nutrients.

Prepare the bone marrow sauce in advance, as it takes about 5 hours to cook. Preheat the oven to 220°C/425°F/gas mark 7.

Place the bones in a roasting tin (pan) and roast in the oven for 30 minutes or until they are well browned. Then transfer the bones to a large saucepan with all the other sauce ingredients and simmer for 3–4 hours.

Sieve the liquid into a smaller saucepan, discarding the bones and vegetables. Allow to boil for about 30 minutes until it becomes a very thick syrup.

Preheat the oven to 230°C/450°F/gas mark 8. Place the rib of beef in a roasting tin (pan), massage in the oil, sprinkle with salt and brown in the oven for 30 minutes.

Turn the temperature down to 160°C/310°F/gas mark 2½ and cook according to how you like your meat. I like the meat quite rare so I cook mine for another 50 minutes; for medium, cook for about 70 minutes; or for well done cook for up to 90 minutes.

While the meat is cooking, prepare the potatoes. In a large oven-proof dish, spread the potato, onion and leek slices in layers. Mix

FOR THE BAKED CREAMY POTATOES
1.2kg (2½lb) potatoes, peeled
   and thinly sliced
1 large onion, thinly sliced
1 leek, thinly sliced
2 eggs
600ml (1 pint/2½ cups) single (light)
   cream
2 cloves of garlic, crushed
1 tsp pink Himalayan salt or sea salt
100g (3½oz/1 cup) freshly grated
   Parmesan cheese
200g (7oz/scant 2 cups) grated Havarti
   or mozzarella cheese

the eggs together with the cream, garlic and salt and pour over the potatoes. Lastly sprinkle the cheeses over the top.

If you have two ovens, preheat the second oven to 180°C/350°F/gas mark 4. If not, turn the oven up to this temperature once you take the beef out of the oven, and allow slightly longer for the baked creamy potatoes to cook.

About 30 minutes before the meat will be ready place the potatoes in the oven to bake for 45 minutes.

When the beef is ready, take out of the oven, cover with foil and allow to rest for at least 15 minutes before carving.

When ready to serve, carve the beef very thinly, serve with the creamy potatoes and the bone marrow sauce, and garnish with herbs if you wish.

This goes well with any vegetables – I particularly like it with green beans, broccoli or kale.

Langtidsbagt Lam med Honning og Sennep

STICKY HONEY AND MUSTARD MARINATED
SLOW-COOKED LEG OF LAMB

SERVES 6

1.5kg (3lb 5oz) leg of lamb (bone in)

2 tbsp sea salt

3 cloves of garlic, sliced

3 sprigs of rosemary, each cut into
   3 pieces

2 tbsp olive oil

6 tbsp honey

6 tbsp wholegrain mustard

Getting me to eat lamb, particularly as a child, was a real challenge. Every time lamb was prepared I would politely have a small taste, smaller than the size of a chocolate chip that is... and swallow very quickly. Then I tried this sticky, slow-cooked lamb, which is, quite simply, to die for...

Any lamb dish, infused with garlic and rosemary, is delicious to me, but this honey and mustard version is my favourite, inspired by a meal I thoroughly enjoyed many years ago in Greece.

Preheat the oven to 220°C/425°F/gas mark 7.

Place the leg of lamb in a roasting tin (pan) and cut lots of deep slashes in the lamb. Fill each slash with some sea salt, a few slices of garlic and a small sprig of rosemary. Drizzle with the olive oil.

Put the lamb in the oven and cook for 30 minutes, then take the lamb out of the oven and turn the oven down to 180°C/350°F/gas mark 4. Carefully put the leg of lamb onto a large piece of foil and fold it up into a parcel. Return to the oven and cook for 3 hours.

Mix together the honey and mustard, then spread it all over the top of the leg of lamb. Return to the oven for 30 minutes, basting the meat with the honey and mustard pan juices every 10 minutes until ready.

The lamb should be well marinated and succulent, with a crispy skin and fall apart easily when carved. This goes particularly well with roasted potatoes or rice.

Får i Kål

LAMB WRAPPED IN A CABBAGE PARCEL

SERVES 8

FOR THE LAMB PARCELS

1 large green cabbage (Savoy works well)

500g (1lb 2oz) minced (ground) lamb

1 egg

1 onion, grated

1 clove of garlic, crushed

2 tbsp oats

1 tsp pink Himalayan salt or sea salt

freshly ground black pepper

2 tbsp olive oil

1 tbsp butter

100ml (3½fl oz/scant ½ cup) marsala

TO SERVE

roughly chopped parsley, to garnish

boiled potatoes or kale and quinoa salad
  (see page 93)

I always use my most beloved possession, a beautiful cooking pot given to me by my grandmother, when I make this particular dish. Each time we came to visit my grandmother from England, all through my childhood, she would make this for us on our first evening in Denmark. It is an extraordinary flavour of my childhood memories of time spent with her.

You can adapt this recipe to suit your own taste – minced (ground) chicken, beef or pork all work really well in these parcels. My darling grandmother also likes to add a little sprinkle of sugar on top of each cabbage parcel for sweetness.

Carefully remove 8 large or 16 small cabbage leaves without breaking them. Place in a large bowl or saucepan, cover with boiling water and leave for a few minutes until they are soft. Reserve 200ml (7fl oz/generous ¾ cup) of the cabbage water and place the leaves on kitchen towel to dry. You may need to cut out the stiff centres.

Mix the minced (ground) lamb with the egg, onion, garlic and oats. Season with salt and pepper. Open a cabbage leaf and fill the middle with a tablespoon of the mince mixture. Fold the cabbage leaf around the mince and tie with cooking string. Repeat with the rest of the cabbage leaves and minced (ground) lamb.

Heat the olive oil and butter in a frying pan (skillet) over a medium heat and brown the cabbage parcels for 5 minutes on each side. Remove the lamb parcels, add the marsala and bring to a simmer, allowing the alcohol to 'burn off'. Return the lamb parcels to the pan and heat for 2 minutes, garnish with parsley, then serve straight away.

Serve with boiled potatoes for a very classic Danish dish, or for a more modern take with my kale and quinoa salad (see page 93).

TIP

— You will need cooking string to tie up these parcels.

Lammefrikadeller

LAMB MEATBALLS WITH PARSLEY, OLIVES,
RED (BELL) PEPPERS AND FETA

132 SERVES 6

FOR THE MEATBALLS
500g (1lb 2oz) minced (ground) lamb
1 red onion, quartered
2 large cloves of garlic
20g (¾oz/¼ cup) breadcrumbs or oats
2 tbsp parsley, plus extra to garnish
80g (3oz) red (bell) pepper, chopped
80g (3oz) feta cheese
16 pitted black olives (optional)
1 egg
½ tsp salt

TO FRY THE MEATBALLS
3 tbsp olive oil
15g (½oz/1 tbsp) butter

It took most of my childhood and youth to understand and grow to like the taste of lamb – this feeling has fortunately changed completely, and my love of lamb has grown very organically. I do, however, still need it to be seasoned well so that the lamb taste is as subtle as possible. This dish is a great way of doing just that, and it's also very popular with children. It is perfect for picnics, in which case it's a good idea to double the quantities, or as a canapé to go with cocktails before dinner.

Put all the meatball ingredients into a food processor and process for a few minutes, or mix the meat in a mixing bowl with all the ingredients hand chopped for a less smooth consistency. Shape the mix into 24 oval balls.

Heat the oil and butter in a large frying pan (skillet) and fry the meatballs for 3–4 minutes on each side until cooked through. Garnish with chopped parsley.

Eat hot or cold with my chickpea salad (see page 94); red cabbage (see page 143) or pickled cucumber (see page 134); or simply serve with freshly baked rye bread (see page 208).

Gammeldags Kylling med Syltede Agurker og Sovs

OLD-FASHIONED CHICKEN WITH PICKLED CUCUMBER
AND A CREAMY WHITE WINE SAUCE

134

SERVES 8

FOR THE OLD-FASHIONED CHICKEN
1 large, good-quality chicken
1 lemon, chopped into chunks
1 bunch of parsley
2 tbsp olive oil
1 tbsp pink Himalayan salt or sea salt
1 whole garlic bulb, halved

FOR THE PICKLED CUCUMBER
2 cucumbers
200ml (7fl oz/generous ¾ cup)
    apple cider vinegar
2 tbsp pink Himalayan salt or sea salt
1 tbsp mustard seeds
2 tbsp sugar (optional)
1 tbsp dill tops
50ml (2fl oz/scant ¼ cup) freshly
    boiled water

FOR THE CREAMY WHITE WINE SAUCE
25g (1oz/2 tbsp) butter
2 tbsp plain (all-purpose) flour
200ml (7fl oz/generous ¾ cup)
    chicken stock
100ml (3½fl oz/scant ½ cup)
    soured cream
50ml (2fl oz/scant ¼ cup) white wine
½ tsp chervil
½ tsp salt
1 tbsp lemon juice

TO SERVE
baked creamy potatoes (see page 127)

This dish has a very special place in my heart. It's the meal that was served every year for my Daddy's birthday since he was a child, and I have had it 41 years in a row for his birthday, even when we were not together. We will continue to make this dish every year on the 15th of May in loving memory of my father.

It is just adorable in my mind that a dish, like so many in this book, can have such a deep meaning and be served on the same day at the same time year after year after year – this continuity is a very important element in the Danish mentality and within our traditions.

First make the pickled cucumber. Peel the cucumbers, then slice very thinly into rings. Put the rings in a large pickling jar. Mix all the other ingredients together, adding the boiled water at the end, and pour over the cucumber. Close the lid once the water has cooled and turn the jar upside-down a few times. Place in the fridge to chill.

Preheat the oven to 220°C/425°F/gas mark 7.

Wash the chicken, pat dry and stuff with the lemon and parsley. Massage the chicken with the oil and salt and place in a roasting tin (pan) with the garlic. Place in the hot oven for 15 minutes.

Turn the oven temperature down to 200°C/400°F/gas mark 6 and roast for an hour. Check the chicken is cooked by inserting a skewer into the thickest part of the leg – if the juices run clear it is cooked. Take the chicken out and leave to rest for 10 minutes before carving.

Make the white sauce by melting the butter in a saucepan. Add the flour, stir, and cook for a few minutes. Next add the chicken stock, followed by the soured cream, stirring continuously. Lastly add the white wine, chervil, salt and lemon juice and simmer for 5 minutes.

Serve the chicken with the baked creamy potatoes, pickled cucumber and white wine sauce.

Ristaffel

RAINBOW CHICKEN CURRY

SERVES 6

FOR THE CHICKEN CURRY

1 tbsp coconut oil

1 red onion, finely chopped

1 clove of garlic, finely chopped

1 tsp tomato purée (paste)

1 tsp pink Himalayan salt or sea salt

2 tbsp curry powder (or 1 tbsp cumin,
  1 tbsp ground turmeric and 1 tbsp
  ground cinnamon)

1 small sweet apple, peeled, cored
  and cut into cubes

1 banana, cut into small cubes

500ml (18fl oz/2 cups) coconut milk

200–300ml (7–10fl oz/generous
  ¾–1¼ cups) chicken stock

600g (1lb 5oz) skinless chicken
  breast, cut into thin strips

FOR THE SIDE DISHES

300g (10½oz/1½ cups) basmati rice

1 tsp salt

6 rashers (slices) of smoked bacon

2 tangerines, peeled and finely chopped

1 banana, thinly sliced

20g (¾oz/¼ cup) desiccated coconut

30g (1¼oz/⅓ cup) almond flakes

30g (1¼oz/3 tbsp) raisins

1 sweet apple, peeled, cored and cubed

100g (3½oz) pineapple, cubed

mango chutney

I don't remember exactly when I first tried this, although I do remember it was with my late and deeply adored cousin Knirke. It was very early on in my childhood and was the first time I had tasted something so 'exotic'. It is interesting how *ristaffel* has really made its way into the homes of many Danes, with the recipes varying in which spices or meats are used. I adore it with chicken, others love it with turkey, or you can use ham or pork. This is a great everyday dish and also super for when you are entertaining as you can prepare most of it in advance. I also find this version is particularly popular with children, and you can be as creative as you like with your toppings – there are no limits.

In a large saucepan, melt the coconut oil, then gently fry the onion and garlic. Add the tomato purée (paste) and salt and stir well. Now add the curry powder and allow it to 'burn off', then add the apple and banana.

Pour in the coconut milk and bring to a simmer. Turn the heat down and simmer for 15 minutes, then remove from the heat, carefully pour into a blender or food processor and blend until smooth.

Return the curry sauce to the saucepan and slowly add the chicken stock, stirring – the sauce should be nice and thick. Now add the chicken strips and cook for another 10 minutes over a medium heat.

While the chicken curry is cooking, rinse the rice under cold running water, then place in a saucepan, cover with water, add the salt and bring to the boil. Boil for 20 minutes. Meanwhile, fry the bacon in a frying pan (skillet) until crispy. Drain on kitchen towel, chop into chunks and put in a small bowl.

Put each of the remaining side dishes into small individual bowls. Serve the chicken curry on a bed of rice. Place all the side dishes on the table so everyone can help themselves to the accompaniments they want.

Poussingryde med Agurksalat

POUSSIN CASSEROLE
WITH CUCUMBER SALAD

SERVES 4

FOR THE POUSSIN CASSEROLE

2 poussins

4 tbsp olive oil

2 tbsp citrus herb salt

1 tbsp butter

2 small red onions, thinly sliced

1 tbsp plain (all-purpose) flour

500ml (18fl oz/2 cups) chicken stock

200ml (7fl oz/generous ¾ cup) single
   (light) cream

100ml (3½fl oz/scant ½ cup) white wine

2 tbsp chopped tarragon

1 tsp Dijon mustard

½ tsp pink Himalayan salt or sea salt

3 large carrots, peeled and cut into
   thick slices

FOR THE CUCUMBER SALAD

1 whole round (butterhead) lettuce

1 cucumber

12 baby pickled onions

FOR THE DRESSING

6 tbsp olive oil

1 tbsp grainy mustard

1 tbsp white wine vinegar

¼ tsp pink Himalayan salt or sea salt

2 tbsp single (light) cream

Old-fashioned roast chicken with cucumber salad and white sauce was always my father's birthday dinner. So simple, and yet through all his 78 years, it was his favourite dish. I have lots of variations on that classic dish, as all my family love it. Here I have swapped a chicken for two poussins, but you can use chicken if you prefer. I mainly serve this casserole in the winter months as it is so delicious, comforting and cosy. Tarragon is a herb I adore, and the way it infuses in this dish is sensational!

Preheat the oven to 250°C/480°F/gas mark 9.

Put the poussins into a large roasting tin (pan), drizzle with half the olive oil (2 tbsp) and sprinkle over the citrus herb salt. Roast in the oven for 20 minutes.

Meanwhile, in a large, heavy-based lidded casserole pot, melt the butter with the rest of the olive oil. Gently fry the onion until soft, then sieve the flour over the onion, mix well and add the stock. Bring the stock to boiling point, then turn down the heat and add the cream, white wine, tarragon, mustard and salt, and stir well.

Remove the poussins from the oven and carefully lower them into the sauce in the casserole pot. Add the carrot, place the lid back on and simmer on the hob (stovetop) for 45 minutes, turning the poussins a couple of times.

Chop the lettuce into pieces and place in a salad bowl. Using a potato peeler, peel the cucumber lengthways to make long, thin strips, then add to the salad along with the baby pickled onions.

Make the dressing by shaking all the dressing ingredients together in a screwtop jar. Carve the poussins, drizzle the salad dressing over the cucumber salad and serve both straight away.

Juleand med det Hele

CHRISTMAS DUCK WITH ALL THE TRIMMINGS

SERVES 4–8

FOR THE DUCK

1 or 2 ducks (4kg/9lb)

2 tbsp salt

2 Cox's apples, cut into chunks

1 red onion

2 sprigs of thyme

FOR THE BONE MARROW SAUCE

2kg (4½lb) beef or veal bones, some
    with bone marrow (ask your butcher)

4 carrots, cut into chunks

1 large onion, skin on, quartered

1 leek, cut into chunks

1 whole garlic bulb, halved

4 tomatoes, halved

1 bouquet garni

2 tsp pink Himalayan salt or sea salt

7 litres (12 pints/30 cups) water

1 bay leaf

2 tbsp red wine

This is a dish I can taste just by closing my eyes. I could eat this each and every day of my life. I adore everything about Christmas, especially in Denmark. It's all about *hygge*, being so cosy, happy and warm. Candles burn constantly, the fire is lit, music hums in the background, family and friends' voices talk excitedly, and there are the most extraordinary smells that change during the day depending on what is being prepared. In the words of Roy Wood's Wizzard: 'Oh I wish it could be Christmas every day…'

The Christmas table is a big deal in our family, and it takes hours to decorate with a Christmas town in the centre on cotton wool (to look like snow) with lots of small china houses with candles inside, fir trees and little elves in beautiful clothes. The whole house smells of cinnamon, cloves and oranges, candles are twinkling everywhere, the table is dressed with silver, cut-glass and Christmas china, ready for this incredible meal.

Ideally make the bone marrow sauce the day before eating.

For the bone marrow sauce
Preheat the oven to 200°C/400°F/gas mark 6.

Place the bones in a roasting tin (pan) and brown in the oven for 30 minutes. Transfer the bones to a very large lidded saucepan with the other sauce ingredients and simmer, with the lid on, for 5 hours.

Sieve the liquid into a smaller saucepan, discarding the bones and vegetables. Bring back to the boil and boil for 1 hour without a lid until it becomes a very thick syrup.

For the duck
Preheat the oven to 200°C/400°F/gas mark 6.

Take your time and massage the salt into the duck really well, massaging the inside and outside of the duck – the better you massage, the crispier the skin will be.

Put the duck into a large roasting tin (pan) and stuff the cavity with the apples, red onion and thyme.

Put the duck into the oven and cook for 15 minutes at the high heat, then turn the temperature down to 150°C/300°F/gas mark 2 and cook for a further 3 hours, every so often pouring away the liquid and fat (reserving the fat – see Tip). Remove from the oven and cover with foil to keep warm.

For the red cabbage
Prepare the cabbage by cutting it in half, removing and discarding the white stem. Chop into very thin slices, wash well, then drain on kitchen towel.

Warm the duck fat in a small saucepan over a low heat, then add the apple and leave to simmer.

Put the red cabbage in a large saucepan. Pour over the blackcurrant cordial, red wine and sugar and bring to the boil, then turn down the heat and simmer for 15 minutes. Next add the apple cider vinegar and salt and cook for a further 20 minutes. Lastly add the simmered apple and season with salt and pepper.

For the caramelized potatoes
Put the potatoes in a saucepan with the salt and cover with water. Bring to the boil and boil for 20 minutes, then drain. Leave to cool, then peel off the skins.

In a large, heavy-bottomed saucepan, melt the sugar very slowly over a low heat. This takes a little while. When the sugar has melted, stir it, and when it becomes golden and starts to bubble a little, add the butter and then the potatoes (they have to be damp) and cook until they are covered in the delicious caramel sauce and warmed through.

To serve, carve the goose on a large wooden chopping board with a very sharp knife and fork. Put the caramelized potatoes and red cabbage into serving dishes, the bone marrow sauce into a gravy boat, and let everyone help themselves to some delicious duck with the potatoes and red cabbage on the side, and the sauce on top.

TIP
– The duck fat is incredible to keep and use later, whether for roasting potatoes or added to fried onions and salt and used as a spread on rye bread.

FOR THE RED CABBAGE
1 whole red cabbage
1 tbsp duck fat (reserved from the cooked duck)
1 small Cox's apple, peeled, cored and finely chopped
200ml (7fl oz/generous ¾ cup) blackcurrant cordial
600ml (1 pint/2½ cups) red wine
2 tbsp sugar
200ml (7fl oz/generous ¾ cup) apple cider vinegar
2 tsp salt
freshly ground black pepper

FOR THE CARAMELIZED POTATOES
500g (1lb 2oz) small new potatoes
1 tsp salt
4 tbsp sugar
25g (1oz/2 tbsp) butter

Fasan Ragout

PHEASANT RAGOUT

SERVES 6

FOR THE RAGOUT

1 whole pheasant, about 500g (1lb 2oz)

1 tbsp butter

2 tbsp olive oil

1 large red onion, finely chopped

2 large cloves of garlic, thinly sliced

2 tbsp tomato purée (paste)

½ tsp pink Himalayan salt or sea salt

10 brown button mushrooms, washed
   and quartered

2 large carrots, thinly sliced (peeled
   or unpeeled)

1 small aubergine (eggplant), cut into
   small dice

6 rashers (slices) of smoked streaky
   bacon, thinly sliced

200ml (7fl oz/generous ¾ cup)
   chicken stock

400ml (13½fl oz/1⅔ cups)
   tomato passata

1 bay leaf

150ml (5fl oz/⅔ cup) red wine

Living in Denmark on 'a farm', aka 'stately home', where we rear pheasants, means that we have always been very creative with this bird. While I adore smoked pheasant breast (see page 31) for breakfast, lunch or dinner, I also find pancakes stuffed with a good creamy pheasant and mushroom mixture quite delicious. This ragout can be eaten with rice, pasta or potatoes, or also stuffed into Chinese-style pancakes or Mexican wraps, served with guacamole, sour cream, salsa and grated cheese, which is a huge hit with my children.

Preheat the oven to 200°C/400°F/gas mark 6.

Put the pheasant in a roasting tin (pan) and place in the oven for 15 minutes.

Meanwhile, in a large lidded casserole pot, melt the butter over a medium heat, then add the olive oil. Add the onion and garlic and gently fry until browned. Then add the tomato purée (paste) and 'burn it off'. Add the salt, mushrooms, carrots, aubergine (eggplant) and bacon and cook for about 5 minutes, stirring.

Next add the stock, passata, bay leaf and wine, and stir well. After the pheasant has cooked for 15 minutes, remove from the oven and carefully add it to the casserole dish, placing the lid back on the dish.

Simmer the ragout gently on the hob (stovetop) for 1½ hours. Take off the heat, remove the pheasant carefully from the pot and place on a chopping board. When cool, using a fork, pull off the meat and shred it, then put the meat back into the casserole dish and simmer for a further 20 minutes.

Serve the ragout with mashed potatoes or rice, or inside savoury pancakes. It's also absolutely delicious served with pasta and Parmesan on top. The leftovers can be used for a second version.

Chapter Five

Main Courses:
Fish and Vegetarian

Laks med Asparges

BAKED SALMON WITH ASPARAGUS
AND ROASTED SWEET POTATOES

SERVES 6

I caught my first salmon on a line in Ireland when I was 18; and my first on a fly in Scotland when I was 25. That was when my feelings for fishing grew to become a great love. I have since fished in Iceland, New Zealand and the Seychelles, as well as the Okavanga Delta, where I wore out my socks 'fighting' to land a fish.

Salmon has become such a popular fish for the Danes, especially in the last two decades. A great way of serving it is with asparagus – the flavours complement each other so well – and I even enjoy this for breakfast on a regular basis. I prefer to use sweet potatoes rather than normal potatoes because of their wonderful taste and the fact they are much higher in vitamin C.

FOR THE SALMON

1 tsp pink Himalayan salt or sea salt

12 green asparagus spears, bottoms trimmed

800g (1lb 12oz) skinned salmon fillet, cut into 18 x 1cm (½ inch) slices

olive oil, to drizzle

FOR THE SWEET POTATOES

6 small sweet potatoes, white or pink fleshed

100ml (3½fl oz/scant ½ cup) olive oil

1 tsp dried thyme

½ tsp sea salt

FOR THE GREEN SAUCE

4 large tbsp mayonnaise

1 tbsp finely chopped dill

1 tbsp finely chopped parsley

1 tbsp finely chopped tarragon

1 tbsp finely chopped chervil

1 tbsp finely chopped chives

1 large clove of garlic, crushed

1 tbsp lemon juice

1 tbsp tarragon vinegar (you can make your own by infusing fresh tarragon in vinegar)

½ tsp Dijon mustard

2 tbsp crème fraîche

½ tsp salt

TO GARNISH

fresh herbs such as dill and parsley

Mix all the ingredients for the green sauce together and set aside in the fridge. This is best made a few hours before serving.

Preheat the oven to 200°C/400°F/gas mark 6.

Peel the sweet potatoes, cut off wedge-size ends, then cut the rest of the sweet potato into wedges and place in a large mixing bowl. Drizzle over the oil, and sprinkle over the thyme and salt, then massage the potatoes so they are well coated. Place on a large baking tray (sheet) and bake in the oven for 50 minutes.

While the potatoes are cooking, bring a saucepan of water to the boil, add the salt and asparagus, cook for 2 minutes and then drain.

Lay 3 slices of salmon next to each other, then put 2 blanched asparagus in the middle across the slices of salmon and wrap the salmon up around the asparagus in a roll (tie with cooking string if it won't stay in a roll). Repeat with the rest of the salmon and asparagus, put in an ovenproof baking dish, drizzle with oil and bake in the oven for 20 minutes.

Serve the fish, potatoes and green sauce together, garnished with fresh herbs of your choice.

Fiskefilet med Hvidvinssovs og Brasede Kartofler

BREADED PLAICE WITH WHITE WINE SAUCE
AND SAUTÉED POTATOES

SERVES 6

FOR THE PLAICE
12 plaice fillets
2 eggs
2 tbsp plain (all-purpose) flour
6 tbsp breadcrumbs
1 tsp salt
2 tbsp butter

FOR THE POTATOES
600g (1lb 5oz) potatoes
2 tbsp salted butter
½ tsp pink Himalayan salt or sea salt

FOR THE WHITE WINE SAUCE
1 tbsp olive oil
1 small yellow onion, finely chopped
250ml (8½fl oz/1 cup) white wine
200ml (7fl oz/generous ¾ cup)
   vegetable stock
12 whole black peppercorns
60g (2oz/¼ cup/½ stick) very cold
   salted butter, cut into chunks

TO SERVE
parsley, to garnish
pink Himalayan salt or sea salt
1 lemon, cut into 6 wedges (optional)

Breaded plaice with white wine sauce is an awesome casual evening dish, served with sautéed potatoes.

Fiskefilet med remoulade (breaded plaice with remoulade) is also a fantastic topping for an open sandwich: plaice served with freshly baked, buttered rye bread, a squeeze of lemon juice and a dollop of remoulade (see page 158) on top. I have yet to come across a child who doesn't enjoy this classic Danish dish – even children who normally refuse to eat fish, love it.

Preheat the oven to 150°C/300°F/gas mark 2. Put the potatoes into a large saucepan filled with salted cold water and bring to the boil, then boil for 10 minutes. Drain and leave to cool. When cold, cut the potatoes into small chunks.

Wash the fish fillets and pat dry with kitchen towel. Crack the eggs into a deep bowl and beat well. Put the flour, breadcrumbs and salt into another deep bowl and mix well. Coat each fish fillet first in the egg mixture and then in the flour and breadcrumb mixture.

Melt the butter in a large frying pan (skillet) and fry the fish fillets in batches for about 3 minutes on each side. Keep warm in the oven.

In another large frying pan (skillet), fry the potatoes. Melt the butter, then add the potatoes, sprinkle with the salt and fry for about 20 minutes until golden and crispy, turning them occasionally.

Meanwhile, make the white wine sauce. Heat the oil in a saucepan and lightly fry the onion. Add the white wine, stock and pepper-corns and heat until it starts to boil, then turn down the heat and gently simmer for 30 minutes. Remove from the heat and add the butter slowly, stirring all the time until combined.

Serve 2 fish fillets per person, with the sautéed potatoes and white wine sauce. Sprinkle over some parsley and extra pink Himalayan salt and enjoy hot, with a wedge of lemon if you wish.

Bagt Torsk med Sennepssovs

BAKED COD WITH MUSTARD SAUCE

SERVES 6

FOR THE COD

6 x 200g (7oz) boneless cod fillets,
    skin on
2 courgettes (zucchini), cut into sticks
200g (7oz) trimmed fine green beans
200g (7oz) trimmed mange tout
    (snow peas)
100g (3½oz/3 cups) spinach leaves
100ml (3½fl oz/scant ½ cup) olive oil
1 tsp pink Himalayan salt or sea salt

FOR THE MUSTARD SAUCE

25g (1oz/2 tbsp) salted butter
2 tbsp plain (all-purpose) flour
250ml (8½fl oz/1 cup) vegetable
    or chicken stock
2 tbsp Dijon mustard
150ml (5fl oz/⅔ cup) single (light) cream
¼ tsp pink Himalayan salt or sea salt

TO SERVE

4 tbsp grated fresh horseradish
4 tbsp pickled beetroot,
    cut into small cubes
2 hard-boiled eggs, whites and yolk
    separated, each finely chopped
4 tbsp chopped parsley

When I hear the word 'cod', I always think of my darling grandfather and him saying 'to be eaten all the months that end with an r' – so September, October, November and December. I always send loving thoughts to him when I make this very traditional fish dish, or any cod dish, as it's his favourite fish.

Preheat the oven to 200°C/400°F/gas mark 6. Cut 6 squares of foil, each about 30cm (12 inches) square.

Meanwhile, place 1 piece of cod onto the centre of each piece of foil. Divide the vegetables equally into 6 mixed vegetable piles. Put 1 pile of vegetables onto each slice of cod, drizzle with the olive oil and sprinkle with the salt. Wrap each piece of foil up into a parcel around the fish and vegetables, making sure there are no gaps. Place on a baking tray (sheet) and bake in the oven for 15 minutes.

Next make the mustard sauce. In a saucepan, melt the butter over a low heat. Sieve in the flour and cook for a couple of minutes, stirring, then slowly pour in the stock, stirring. When mixed well, add the mustard and cream, and bring to a gentle boil. Season with salt.

Serve each person a portion of vegetables and cod. Sprinkle a little horseradish, beetroot, egg and parsley over the fish, then add the mustard sauce. This also goes well with boiled new potatoes.

Dampet Hellefisk Serveret Kold med Grønsovs

CHILLED HALIBUT WITH A COLD GREEN HERB SAUCE

SERVES 6

FOR THE HALIBUT
1 bunch of lemon balm
1 bunch of tarragon
900g (2lb) halibut fillets
2 tsp pink Himalayan salt or sea salt

FOR THE COLD GREEN HERB SAUCE
200g (7oz/generous ¾ cup) mayonnaise
150g (5½oz/⅔ cup) crème fraîche
1 tbsp tarragon
2 tbsp coriander (cilantro)
1 tbsp chervil
2 tbsp watercress
2 tbsp rocket (arugula)
2 tbsp spinach leaves
3 tbsp lemon juice
1 tsp pink Himalayan salt or sea salt

FOR THE NEW POTATOES
500g (1lb 2oz) new potatoes
1 tsp salt
1 tbsp butter
1 tbsp chopped parsley

TO SERVE
lemon quarters

My father had a fantastic cook called Finn for many years, an utterly brilliant chef in so many ways. My father was an amazing cook himself, but who doesn't like a break now and again? Probably everyone but me! I have been known to go into restaurant kitchens when abroad and start helping, or just to learn about another country's kitchen. It's bizarre, but cooking is so deep in my bones I just can't help myself, I miss it too much, it's my oxygen.

This dish is awesome for summer nights, sitting outside under the stars and incredible Northern lights of Scandinavia, or to enjoy in your garden, or on your terrace or balcony.

Place the lemon balm and tarragon into a fish steamer (or other steamer), then add the halibut fillets on top. Season with the salt and steam for approximately 15 minutes. Remove the fish from the steamer and place in the fridge to chill for an hour, which firms the flesh completely.

To make the cold green herb sauce, blend all the sauce ingredients together in a blender or food processor, then put in the fridge to chill until needed.

Place the new potatoes and salt in a saucepan with enough water to cover the potatoes. Turn on the heat to high, bring to the boil, then cook over a medium heat before draining. They will take 20 minutes from the start of cooking.

Melt the butter in a saucepan, add the parsley, then pour over the potatoes and toss well to coat. Serve the warm potatoes with the cold fish, cold herb sauce and lemon quarters to squeeze over.

Fiskefrikadeller med Remoulade
FISH BALLS WITH REMOULADE

SERVES 4

Fish balls are probably a favourite for most Danish families. We have fishmongers in almost every harbour, and these tasty balls are freshly made there, to eat on the go or to be devoured elsewhere. You can also buy the ready-made mixture and then cook them at home.

In my family we have always made these fish balls from scratch. They are fabulous for dinner served with new potatoes, remoulade and a slice of lemon; for lunch with freshly baked, buttered rye bread with the remoulade on the side; or for breakfast with scrambled eggs or with avocado on toasted rye bread – take your pick of time of day to enjoy them.

FOR THE FISH BALLS

200g (7oz) skinless salmon fillet

200g (7oz) skinless cod fillet

1 tsp pink Himalayan salt or sea salt

2 tbsp plain (all-purpose) flour

2 tbsp potato flour

150ml (5fl oz/⅔ cup) milk

1 egg

1 small yellow onion

1 tbsp chives

2 tbsp olive oil

20g (¾oz/1½ tbsp) salted butter

To make the fish balls, put all the ingredients, except the olive oil and butter, into a blender and blend well. Put in a bowl to rest while you make the remoulade.

FOR THE REMOULADE

8 tbsp mayonnaise

25g (1oz/⅛ cup) capers, finely chopped

50g (1¾oz/⅓ cup) cornichons, finely chopped

50g (1¾oz) pickled onions, chopped, or ¼ red onion, very finely chopped

½ carrot, very finely chopped

2 tbsp apple cider vinegar

1 tsp mustard

1 tsp dried tarragon

½ tsp ground turmeric

1 tbsp olive oil

To make the remoulade, either mix all the ingredients together in a bowl, or if you prefer it smoother (which my children do), place all the ingredients in a blender or food processor and blend until smooth and there are no bits.

Put the new potatoes into a saucepan and cover with water. Add the salt and simmer for 20 minutes, then turn off the heat. The potatoes can stay like this all day long and will still have an excellent consistency, so just drain when ready to serve.

To form the fish balls, take a spoonful of the mix and shape in your hand into a ball shape – you should make about 12 balls.

FOR THE NEW POTATOES

300g (10½oz) new baby potatoes

1 tsp salt

Heat the olive oil and butter in a frying pan (skillet) and fry the fish balls over a medium–low heat for about 10 minutes in total, turning occasionally so each side is golden.

TO GARNISH

chopped chives

Serve the fish balls hot with the new potatoes, a generous spoonful of remoulade and a sprinkle of chopped chives.

Spaghetti med Tunfiskesovs

MY FATHER'S SUNDAY SPAGHETTI WITH TUNA FISH SAUCE

SERVES 6

All my life, this has been a very popular and deeply loved special family dish – and when we were very lucky, it wasn't just served on Sundays! Today, each of my family have their own way of making this, but all inspired by my father's original dish, which he learned from his family's cook when he was a child. I love this, and hope you and your family and friends will love it too… It truly is my father in a dish.

FOR THE TUNA FISH SAUCE
3 tbsp olive oil

1 onion, very finely chopped

1 clove of garlic, very finely chopped

2 tbsp tomato purée (paste)

300ml (10fl oz/1¼ cups) tomato passata

1 tsp pink Himalayan salt or sea salt

300ml (10fl oz/1⅓ cups) single (light) cream

6 basil leaves, torn

3 tbsp tomato ketchup (or more for sweetness; especially for the kids)

400–500g (14oz–1lb 2oz) tuna fillets in olive oil (I like Brindisa Ortiz and use 2 x 220g (8oz) jars)

freshly ground black pepper

FOR THE PASTA
2 tsp salt

500g (1lb 2oz) dried spaghetti

drizzle of olive oil

TO SERVE
basil leaves, to garnish

200g (7oz/2 cups) freshly grated Parmesan cheese

In a saucepan over a medium heat, heat the olive oil, then add the onion and garlic and gently fry until they are almost transparent. Add the tomato purée (paste) and simmer for a few minutes – you will see the colour change. Now add the tomato passata and salt, and leave to gently simmer for a few minutes.

Over a low heat, add the cream slowly, stirring continuously, but make sure you don't let the sauce boil. Add the basil leaves and simmer for another minute, then add the tomato ketchup. Taste and season with salt and pepper. The sauce should have the perfect creamy flavour now, so add the tuna fish and allow to simmer on a low heat for 5 minutes to properly heat through.

While the sauce is cooking, bring a large saucepan filled with water to the boil, adding the salt. Add the pasta and boil according to the packet instructions or your taste (my family like it al dente). Drain, then put into a large bowl and drizzle with olive oil.

Pour the tuna sauce over the pasta and mix so all the pasta is well covered. Transfer to a serving dish and serve immediately with extra basil leaves and grated Parmesan cheese.

Min Families Skaldyrsgryde

MY FAMILY'S SHELLFISH STEW

SERVES 6–8

FOR THE BASE OF THE STEW

3 tbsp olive oil

1 large red onion, finely chopped

2 large cloves of garlic, finely chopped

½ fennel bulb, thinly sliced

1 tbsp tomato purée (paste)

300g (10½oz) cherry tomatoes,
   finely chopped

1 tsp pink Himalayan salt or sea salt

2 tbsp finely chopped parsley

1 large carrot, finely chopped

1 stick of celery, finely chopped

1 large pinch of saffron threads, softened
   in 4 tbsp freshly boiled water

200ml (7fl oz/generous ¾ cup)
   white wine

200ml (7fl oz/generous ¾ cup)
   fish stock

2 bay leaves

½ tbsp apple cider vinegar

FOR THE SHELLFISH

200g (7oz) prepared mussels
   (see page 167)

300g (10½oz) skinless monkfish chunks

100g (3½oz) scallops

250g (9oz) raw prawns (shrimp)

100g (3½oz) clams

Being surrounded by water means that the over 400 islands that make up Denmark have a very rich abundance of seafood. The creativity of recipes based around these wonderful seafoods knows no limits. In the world we live in today, travel has meant food preparation is inspired by every country we visit, and this stew can easily be adapted to suit your tastes, your favourite seafood, and what is available. 'The world is your oyster.'

In a large saucepan, gently heat the olive oil over a medium–low heat, then add the onion, garlic and fennel and fry for a couple of minutes. Add the tomato purée (paste) and 'burn it off'. Add the cherry tomatoes and salt and simmer for 15 minutes, then add the parsley and cook for 2 more minutes.

Take the base mix off the heat and blend in a food processor or blender until smooth. Pour back into the saucepan and add the carrot, celery, saffron, white wine, fish stock, bay leaves and apple cider vinegar. Bring back to the boil, then simmer for 10 minutes.

Add the mussels to the stew and simmer for 2 minutes, then add the monkfish and scallops and cook for 2 minutes, gently stirring. Lastly add the prawns (shrimp) and clams and simmer for 5 minutes until everything is cooked and warmed through.

This is lovely served with freshly baked, warm bread on the side.

Dampet Muslinger

STEAMED MUSSELS IN A WHITE WINE
AND CREAM SAUCE

SERVES 6

3kg (6½lb) mussels

2 tbsp olive oil

20g (¾oz/1½ tbsp) butter

2 large cloves of garlic, finely chopped

3 shallots, finely chopped

1 carrot, finely chopped

1 stick of celery, finely chopped

½ fennel bulb, finely chopped

4 tbsp finely chopped parsley

1 tsp pink Himalayan salt or sea salt

1 bay leaf

200ml (7fl oz/generous ¾ cup) white wine

200ml (7fl oz/generous ¾ cup) single
(light) cream

2 tbsp crème fraîche

'Out is good, but home is best' rings through my ears again and again. What I particularly love about Denmark is that it supports home life as being the most important place to invest your time and energy. Office work finishes earlier than in most other countries, school finishes around 1.30pm every day – home time, play time, family time, sports time, time to be doing what really matters with those who really matter. Make your life as good as you can, filled with as much love, laughter and happiness as possible, taking priority of those that really matter – family first and foremost. I think the happiest people in the world are those who have done exactly this, putting family first – nothing else matters in comparison.

How cosy or *hyggelig*, as we say in Denmark, to grab a couple of buckets and walk hand in hand with a parent, grandparent, cousin or friend on the beach, looking for crabs and mussels... treasured moments, special times – this is what life is all about, making special memories with those we love and care for.

First prepare the mussels – clean the shells well, remove the beards, and discard any mussels that are open and do not close when tapped. Finally rinse well under cold running water to get rid of any grit.

In a very large saucepan, heat the olive oil and butter, then add the garlic and shallots and fry for a couple of minutes.

Add the carrot, celery, fennel, parsley and salt and cook, stirring, for another couple of minutes. Then add the bay leaf, white wine and mussels and simmer for 5 minutes, shaking the pan a couple of times. Discard any mussels that have not opened when cooked.

Lastly add the cream and crème fraîche, stir once again, shake and serve. This is delicious with freshly baked, warm, crispy bread.

Kartoffelfad med Bønner

BEAN AND POTATO CASSEROLE

SERVES 6

FOR THE BEANS

50g (1¾oz/¼ cup) dried kidney beans

50g (1¾oz/¼ cup) dried butter
(lima) beans

50g (1¾oz/¼ cup) dried black-eyed beans

FOR THE CASSEROLE

4 tbsp olive oil

1 large onion, chopped

1 large clove of garlic, sliced

1 leek, thinly sliced

1 tbsp tomato purée (paste)

300ml (10fl oz/1¼ cups) tomato passata
or 300g (10½oz) skinless chopped
tomatoes

300ml (10fl oz/1¼ cups) vegetable stock

250g (9oz) new potatoes, cut
into chunks

200g (7oz) carrots, cut into chunks

2 bay leaves

130g (4½oz) grilled (broiled) artichokes,
chopped

16 pitted green olives, thinly sliced

½ tsp pink Himalayan salt or sea salt

100g (3½oz/1 cup) freshly grated
Parmesan cheese

I think I can safely say that a very large proportion of the Danish population eat their main hot meal of the day with potatoes of some variation on the side – boiled, smashed, mashed, baked, fried or gratinated.

Casseroles have always had a great presence in Denmark, especially in the winter months; and this vegetarian version is SO good. I find it utterly satisfying, even for a meat-loving person, but you can always add chicken or another meat if you really want to.

Put the 3 types of dried beans in a bowl, cover with water and leave to soak for 8 hours. Drain the beans, place in a saucepan with fresh water to cover, then bring to the boil and boil for 45 minutes. Drain and set aside.

Preheat the oven to 180°C/350°F/gas mark 4.

In a large saucepan, heat the olive oil and add the onion, garlic and leek. Fry for a couple of minutes, then add the tomato purée (paste) and cook for a few more minutes, then add the tomato passata. Simmer for 10 minutes.

Add the stock, new potatoes, carrots, bay leaves, artichokes, green olives, cooked beans and salt and simmer for another 20 minutes, then transfer to a medium-sized ovenproof dish.

Bake in the oven for 25 minutes, then remove from the oven and sprinkle the Parmesan over the top. Return to the oven and bake for a further 5 minutes.

It is also great fun to cook this for a beach barbecue. Simply simmer the casserole in a large saucepan over a hot fire until cooked, then serve sprinkled with the Parmesan.

Bagte Rodfrugter

ROASTED ROOT VEGETABLES WITH FOUR DANISH CHEESES

SERVES 6–8

FOR THE ROOT VEGETABLES

4 tbsp olive oil

2 red onions, thinly sliced

2 leeks, thinly sliced

2 large sweet potatoes, peeled and
    thinly sliced

1 large butternut squash, skin and pips
    removed, flesh thinly sliced

1 celeriac (celery root), peeled and
    thinly sliced

10 Jerusalem artichokes, skin scraped,
    thinly sliced

FOR THE CREAMY CHEESE SAUCE

40g (1½oz/3 tbsp) butter

2 tbsp plain (all-purpose) flour

500ml (18fl oz/2 cups) single (light)
    cream

300g (10½oz/2⅔ cups) grated Havarti
    cheese

300g (10½oz/2⅔ cups) grated Danbo
    cheese

There is a really funny story about my beloved late mother Margaretha, who ordered some cheese before our big move to the UK in 1982. As far as she was concerned, she had ordered 12 small pieces of ordinary breakfast cheese, Danbo, and 12 small pieces of old cheese, Gammel Ole. A huge delivery lorry drove through the gates to our house, and the men on board unloaded 12 pieces of 40 x 40cm (16 x 16 inch) Danbo and 12 similar pieces of Gammel Ole. To put this into perspective, each piece of cheese weighed about 8kg (17lb), meaning my darling mother had ordered a total of 192kg (over 420lb) of cheese! Fortunately, that didn't stop our love of cheese, and this dish is a winner.

Preheat the oven to 200°C/400°F/gas mark 6.

Heat the olive oil in a frying pan (skillet) and fry the onions and leeks until softened. Layer half the sweet potatoes, butternut squash, celeriac (celery root) and Jerusalem artichokes in a medium-sized ovenproof dish, then add half the fried onions and leeks.

Next make the creamy cheese sauce. Melt the butter in a saucepan, then add the flour and stir well, cooking for a few minutes. Slowly add the cream, whisking consistently so there are no lumps. Finally add the cheeses and continue to cook, stirring, until the cheese has melted and the sauce is smooth.

Pour half the cheese sauce over the layered vegetables, then layer the remaining prepared vegetables and add the rest of the onions and leeks on top. To finish, add the rest of the cheese sauce. Put into the oven and bake for 1 hour, then serve hot.

NOTE
– If you don't have Havarti or Danbo cheeses, then you can use a mix of Cheddar and mozzarella cheese instead.

Oste Soufflé

CHEESE SOUFFLÉ WITH CHEESY BREAD

SERVES 6

I think that if I had to live off just one main protein, I could easily survive on cheese. Like many Danes, I grew up on bread, cheese and butter for breakfast every day. If I'm working late or come home after a great night out, I will, without a doubt, make a pit stop in the kitchen and have a piece of crisp bread with butter and cheese, or a slice of toasted rye bread with cheese and some avocado on the side – it always satisfies any kind of hunger. Cheese soufflé is to me a sophisticated, super simple but slightly more time-consuming version of cheese on toast…

FOR THE CHEESE SOUFFLÉ

75g (2¾oz/⅓ cup/⅔ stick) salted butter

75g (2¾oz/⅔ cup) plain (all-purpose) flour

400ml (13½fl oz/1⅔ cups) milk

6 eggs

¼ tsp ground nutmeg

150g (5½oz/1⅓ cups) grated Havarti cheese, or another full-flavoured hard cheese, e.g. Edam or Cheddar cheese

FOR THE CHEESY BREAD

6 slices of rye bread (or baguette or other bread)

6 tbsp linseed (flaxseed) oil or butter

250g (9oz/generous 2 cups) grated Havarti or Cheddar cheese

TO SERVE

Dijon mustard (optional)

Preheat the oven to 180°C/350°F/gas mark 4. Prepare 6 small ramekins by greasing the insides with a small amount of butter.

To make the soufflé, melt the butter in a saucepan over a low heat, then sieve in the flour and cook, stirring, for a few minutes. Slowly pour in the milk, whisking all the time so there are no lumps. Take off the heat, put into a large mixing bowl and leave to cool.

Separate the eggs, putting the whites into a clean mixing bowl and adding the yolks to the flour and milk mixture. Mix the egg yolks in, then add the nutmeg and grated cheese and mix well again.

Prepare the cheesy bread. Place the 6 slices of bread on a baking tray (sheet), drizzle with the oil or butter, then divide the grated cheese equally between the slices of bread and spread out evenly on top.

Whisk the egg whites with an electric whisk until firm and forming sharp peaks, then fold into the soufflé mixture very carefully. Pour the soufflé mixture into the ramekins, then place straight into the oven and bake for about 30 minutes, adding the cheesy bread after 15 minutes. When cooked, the top of the soufflés should have risen and be nice and golden, and the cheesy bread should be bubbling.

Serve the soufflé immediately so it doesn't collapse, with the cheesy bread and some Dijon mustard on the side if you wish.

Fyldt Bagt Græskar med Ost
STUFFED PUMPKIN WITH NUTS AND DANISH CHEESE

SERVES 6

1 Natoora Delica pumpkin

8 tbsp olive oil

a pinch plus 1 tsp pink Himalayan
salt or sea salt

1 large red onion, finely chopped

1 large clove of garlic, finely chopped

200g (7oz/1½ cups) pine nuts

200g (7oz/1½ cups) water chestnuts,
cubed

2 tbsp hemp seeds

100g (3½oz/¾ cup) cashew nuts

2 tbsp oats

2 tbsp honey

2 tbsp lemon juice

200g (7oz/1¾ cups) grated aged
Havarti or Cheddar cheese

In the good old days, it wasn't a question of: 'Can we eat this pumpkin, or is it just for carving for Halloween?', they were all farmed to eat. I tend to always use the 'pie pumpkins', which can also be used for Halloween if it's that time of year.

Pumpkin is one of my favourite vegetables, even in its most simple form, drizzled with olive oil and coarse sea salt and baked in the oven for an hour – utterly, utterly delicious.

This dish is a really satisfying winter warmer, perfect for a girly dinner, or as a very fulfilling side dish to my pulled pork (see page 68) or roast chicken (see page 134).

Preheat the oven to 200°C/400°F/gas mark 6.

Prepare the pumpkin by cutting a 'lid' out of the top, then scoop out the seeds and discard. Take out the flesh carefully, leaving the skin intact. Chop the pumpkin flesh roughly and place in an ovenproof dish. Drizzle with 4 tbsp of olive oil, season with a pinch of salt and bake in the oven for 30 minutes.

Meanwhile, in a large saucepan, warm the remaining 4 tbsp of olive oil, then add the onion, garlic and the remaining 1 tsp of salt. Gently fry for a couple of minutes, then add the pine nuts, water chestnuts, hemp seeds, cashew nuts, oats and honey. Fry until golden and crispy, then set aside.

When the pumpkin flesh is baked, take it out of the oven and mix in the nut mixture, adding the lemon juice and half the grated cheese.

Turn the temperature down to 180°C/350°F/gas mark 4. Transfer the nut filling into the whole pumpkin and top with the remaining cheese. Bake in the oven for 20 minutes.

Take the pumpkin out of the oven and leave for 10 minutes before cutting it into 6 portions. This is delicious on its own or with my kale and quinoa salad (see page 93) on the side.

Grønkål, Aubergine og Broccoli Fad

KALE, AUBERGINE (EGGPLANT) AND BROCCOLI BAKE

SERVES 6

FOR THE BAKE

200g (7oz/3 cups) chopped kale leaves, stalks discarded

1 broccoli head, cut into small florets

50g (1¾oz/2 cups) basil

1 small aubergine (eggplant), very thinly sliced lengthways

200g (7oz/scant 2 cups) freshly grated Parmesan cheese

200g (7oz/scant 2 cups) grated Havarti, Danbo (or even mozzarella) cheese

FOR THE TOMATO SAUCE

4 tbsp olive oil

1 large red onion, finely chopped

1 litre (1¾ pints/4 cups) passata

1 bay leaf

1 tsp pink Himalayan salt or sea salt

10 basil leaves

'Eating your greens' is tastier now than ever. We are so lucky to be living at a time with such a great understanding of what is good for us – how we can be truly responsible and nourish our bodies and thus our minds. This hearty bake is full of nutrients, and is also a dish that my children adore – inspired by our love of Italian and Turkish cuisines, it's a great combo.

Preheat the oven to 200°C/400°F/gas mark 6.

Start by making the tomato sauce. Heat the olive oil in a small saucepan, add the chopped onion, fry for a couple of minutes, then add the passata, bay leaf and salt and simmer for 15 minutes. Remove and discard the bay leaf, add the basil, transfer to a blender or food processor and blend to a smooth consistency. Divide the sauce equally between 3 jugs or bowls and clean the blender.

In the blender, blend the kale, broccoli and basil until smooth.

Line the bottom of a medium–large ovenproof dish (a lasagne dish works well) with one-third of the tomato sauce.

Place half the aubergine (eggplant) slices on top in one layer, then carefully add half of the blended kale and broccoli mixture on top of the aubergine (eggplant), smoothing it out. Cover with another third of the tomato sauce and then sprinkle half of each cheese over the top.

Repeat the last layers again, using the rest of the ingredients: the aubergine (eggplant), blended kale and broccoli, tomato sauce, finishing with the rest of the cheese.

Bake in the oven for 1 hour and then serve hot.

Chapter Six

Desserts

Pandekager med Jordbær Syltetøj

PANCAKES WITH STRAWBERRY JAM (JELLY)

SERVES 6

FOR THE PANCAKES

500g (1lb 2oz/4 cups) plain
    (all-purpose) flour

2 eggs

¼ tsp salt

1 tsp raw cane sugar

1 tbsp vanilla sugar

1 tsp ground cardamom

800ml (1½ pints/3⅓ cups) milk

butter, for frying

FOR THE STRAWBERRY JAM (JELLY)

500g (1lb 2oz) strawberries, quartered

200g (7oz/1 cup) raw cane sugar

50ml (2fl oz/scant ¼ cup) water

1 tsp gelatine

TO SERVE

raw cane sugar, to sprinkle

One of the things I love about this recipe is the fact that it's my grandmother's favourite dish in the whole wide world, and at least once a week, she has pancakes with strawberry jam for dinner – how cute is that? My beloved grandmother is now 92 years old, so these pancakes have clearly done her a great deal of good!

We already have the tradition in my little family of enjoying pancakes at least once a week, normally on Friday or Saturday. We love to have them with a large spoon of strawberry jam (jelly) spread over the top, and sometimes a scoop of vanilla ice cream or melted Nutella as well – just delicious and so *hyggeligt*.

Ideally start making the strawberry jam (jelly) the day before you want to eat it as this is the best way to get the really intense flavour of the strawberries.

Place the strawberries in a large saucepan with the sugar and leave to sit overnight. The next day, add the measured water and over a medium–high heat bring to the boil, then turn down the heat and simmer for 20 minutes, stirring occasionally. Add the gelatine and stir well, then remove from the heat. You can either serve as a chunky jam (jelly), or my children love the mixture blended to make a smooth jam (jelly).

When you are ready to eat, put all the pancake ingredients, except the butter for frying, into a large bowl and mix well until smooth.

Melt a little butter in a non-stick frying pan (skillet) over a medium heat. Pour in enough batter mixture to just cover two-thirds of the pan. Move the pan around in a swirling motion so the mixture thinly fills the entire pan.

Cook each pancake for about 2 minutes on each side until lightly browned. Place on a plate and wrap in foil to keep warm while you make the rest of the pancakes. Serve the pancakes with the strawberry jam (jelly), sugar to sprinkle, and ice cream if you wish.

Abemad

MONKEY FOOD – FRUIT SALAD WITH VANILLA CREAM AND CHOCOLATE CHUNKS

SERVES 6

FOR THE FRUIT SALAD

4 bananas, halved and sliced

2 large sweet, crispy apples,
    cut into small chunks

1 large crunchy pear, cut into
    small chunks

2 large sweet oranges, cut into
    small chunks

2 tangerines, cut into small chunks

1 small sweet pineapple, cut into
    small chunks

1 sweet mango, cut into small chunks

juice of 1 orange

FOR THE VANILLA CREAM

4 raw pasteurized egg yolks

6 tbsp raw cane sugar

2 vanilla pods (beans), halved
    and seeds scraped

500ml (18fl oz/2 cups) whipping cream

TO TOP

100g (3½oz) dark chocolate, chopped
    roughly into chunks

Easy peasy to make, and almost always possible in most Danish homes – we have fresh fruit, we have cream and we have chocolate … we are just normal human beings! This is a very child-friendly dessert, although I don't know many grown-ups who don't love it just as much as the kids do.

First make the fruit salad. Mix all the chopped fruit together in a large bowl and squeeze the orange juice over the fruit salad.

In a large bowl, whisk the egg yolks with the sugar and vanilla seeds until you get a gorgeous pale yellow creamy mixture.

In a separate bowl, whip the cream with an electric hand mixer until nice and firm. Very gently fold in the egg mixture to the cream.

Serve the fruit salad in deep bowls with the light vanilla cream on top followed by the chocolate chunks.

Rabarbersuppe med Vaniljeis
RHUBARB SOUP WITH VANILLA ICE CREAM

SERVES 6

This beautiful pink soup became an all-time favourite dessert the first time I tasted it about 25 years ago. It is so fresh, delicate and light, yet perfumed like a French cologne and satisfying like good chocolate. Once I start, I cannot stop – I just wish the rhubarb season lasted all year.

I realize it's an investment if you don't already have one, but an ice cream maker may just be the happiest purchase you ever make – I know that mine has been...

FOR THE RHUBARB SOUP
500g (1lb 2oz) rhubarb, cut into
    1cm (½ inch) thick slices
160g (5¾oz/¾ cup) raw cane sugar
1 tbsp vanilla sugar
1 vanilla pod (bean), halved lengthways,
    each half cut into 2 or 3 pieces
1 tbsp lemon juice
800ml (1½ pints/3⅓ cups) water

FOR THE VANILLA ICE CREAM
200ml (7fl oz/generous ¾ cup)
    full-fat (whole) milk
100ml (3½fl oz/scant ½ cup) double
    (heavy) cream
2 egg yolks
160g (5¾oz/¾ cup) raw cane sugar
2 vanilla pods (beans), halved and
    seeds scraped

FOR THE TOASTED ALMONDS
150g (5½oz/1 cup) whole raw almonds
2 tsp butter

First make the vanilla ice cream. In a saucepan over a medium heat, heat the milk and cream until just before it reaches boiling point. Take off the heat and allow to cool.

In a large bowl, mix the egg yolks, sugar and vanilla seeds with an electric hand whisk until a very creamy and pale yellow colour. Add the cooled milk mixture slowly, mix well, then pour into your ice cream maker and follow the manufacturer's instructions.

To make the rhubarb soup, place the rhubarb in a large saucepan and add the sugar, vanilla sugar, vanilla pod pieces, lemon juice and 300ml (10fl oz/1¼ cups) of the water. Bring to the boil, then turn down the heat and gently simmer for 15 minutes.

Using a potato masher, mash the rhubarb. Pour in the remaining measured water and simmer for another 25 minutes. Allow to cool a little and then drain through a sieve into a clean bowl, discarding any rhubarb pieces. Put the clear soup into the fridge to cool.

To prepare the almonds, put them into a bowl of boiling water for a few minutes, then drain and remove the skins. Chop roughly. Melt the butter in a saucepan over a low heat, then add the almonds and cook until they go golden. Remove and dry on kitchen towel.

Pour the rhubarb soup into deep soup bowls, add a scoop of vanilla ice cream in the centre and top with the toasted almond flakes.

Koldskål med Kammerjunkere

COLD BUTTERMILK SOUP
WITH VANILLA AND OAT COOKIES

SERVES 6

My son, Alexander, could live off this dish alone for the rest of his life. It's a traditional summer dessert, although in Alexander's case, it's also breakfast at least twice a week ... bring on summer!

FOR THE COLD BUTTERMILK SOUP
1 egg (optional)
80g (3oz/⅓ cup) raw cane sugar
1 vanilla pod (bean), halved
   and seeds scraped
grated zest and juice of 1 unwaxed lemon
1 litre (1¾ pints/4 cups) buttermilk
1 tsp vanilla sugar

To make the cold buttermilk soup, crack the egg, if using, into a large bowl, beat lightly, then add the sugar and vanilla seeds and stir well.

Next add the lemon zest and juice, stirring constantly. Then add the buttermilk and vanilla sugar, stir well, then put into the fridge to cool.

TO SERVE
kammerjunkere (vanilla and oat cookies)
   (see page 226)

Once chilled, serve the buttermilk in deep bowls with lots of fresh *kammerjunkere* cookies on top.

Ris à L'amande med Kirsebærsovs
RICE PUDDING WITH HOT CHERRY SAUCE

SERVES 10

FOR THE BASIC RICE PUDDING
500g (1lb 2oz/2⅔ cups) pudding rice
   (short-grain white rice)
500ml (18fl oz/2 cups) water
¼ tsp pink Himalayan salt or sea salt
2 litres (3½ pints/8 cups) full-fat
   (whole) milk

FOR THE *RIS À L'AMANDE*
150g (5½oz/1 cup) whole raw almonds
2 vanilla pods (beans), cut in half and
   seeds scraped
2 tbsp vanilla sugar
4 tbsp dark rum
600ml (1 pint/2½ cups) whipping cream

FOR THE CHERRY SAUCE
400g (14oz/scant 3 cups) cherries
300ml (10floz/1¼ cups) water
160g (5¾oz/¾ cup) raw cane sugar
1 tbsp vanilla sugar
1 tbsp cornflour (cornstarch)

Many Danish families will eat *ris à l'amande* for pudding on Christmas Eve – a traditional dessert of cold rice pudding combined with vanilla, almonds and whipped cream and served with a hot cherry sauce. My family are a little different – we eat rice pudding as a starter on Christmas Eve, with cinnamon and sugar on top, or in my father's case, he loved single (light) cream and white sugar. My darling godmother Kirsten often makes rice pudding for my children, as she made it for my sister and I in our childhood.

Here I've given two recipes – the traditional rice pudding is utterly delicious, while the *ris à l'amande* is the perfect dessert for a special occasion. We also have a wonderful tradition of putting one single almond in the mix, and whoever gets the almond gets the 'almond gift' – big joy!

Place the pudding rice in a sieve and rinse well under cold running water. In a large saucepan, bring the measured water to the boil, then add the pudding rice and salt and boil for 2 minutes. Now add the milk and gently simmer for 45 minutes. Keep stirring so the rice doesn't stick to the bottom, then remove from the heat. You can either eat this hot now as rice pudding, or leave to cool then make it into *ris à l'amande*.

Put the almonds in a bowl of boiling water for a couple of minutes so the skin comes off easily, then drain. Once cool, take the skins off and chop the almonds roughly.

Add the vanilla seeds, vanilla sugar, rum and almonds to the rice pudding and mix well. Transfer to a serving bowl and put in the fridge to chill.

When the rice pudding is cold, whisk the cream until thick. Mix the whipped cream into the cold rice pudding, then return to the fridge to chill until ready to serve. This is normally served very cold in Denmark.

To make the cherry sauce, wash the cherries, remove and discard the stones and cut the cherries into quarters. Put into a large saucepan, pour the measured water on top and add the sugar and vanilla sugar. Place over a medium heat until it starts to bubble, then turn down the heat and simmer gently for 30 minutes. Sieve in the cornflour (cornstarch), which will give the sauce a thicker consistency, and mix well.

Serve the very cold rice pudding with the hot cherry sauce on top.

VARIATION

For an alternative to the *ris à l'amande*, follow the basic recipe above. Then, once ready, serve hot and with a lump of cold butter in the middle of your rice pudding and a mixture of sugar and cinnamon sprinkled on top, which is my preferred Christmas variation.

KLATKAGER OR RICE PUDDING SPLODGES

In Denmark we love to use the leftovers of our rice pudding (if there are any!) to make rice pudding splodges (pancakes) the following day. To make the splodges, heat a frying pan (skillet) and add a knob of butter. Once melted, add a large tablespoon of the leftover rice pudding mixture, shape it like a round pancake, and fry on both sides until crispy. Serve with strawberry jam (jelly) (see page 180) and icing (confectioner's) sugar – completely delicious.

194

Mormors Bagte Æbler med Marcipan og Rosiner

GRANNY'S AMAZING BAKED APPLES
WITH MARZIPAN AND RAISINS

SERVES 8

FOR THE APPLES

8 large, crisp Braeburn apples
  (my favourite)

FOR THE MARZIPAN STUFFING

50g (1¾oz/¼ cup/scant ½ stick) butter
50g (1¾oz/⅓ cup) raisins
120g (4oz) marzipan, chopped
8 tsp raw cane sugar
1 tbsp ground cinnamon

FOR THE VANILLA CREAM

3 pasteurized eggs
140g (5oz/scant ¾ cup) raw cane sugar
2 vanilla pods (beans), cut in half
  and seeds scraped
500ml (18fl oz/2 cups) double (heavy)
  cream

My grandmother has the most adorable garden, set in the most adorable bay, on my family's estate. Fond memories of my time there include sitting amongst her raspberry bushes eating huge, juicy berries; collecting cucumbers and tomatoes before lunch; or climbing her wonderful apple tree or pear tree. The apples always seemed never-ending, and many feasts were created using these delicious fruits. These baked apples have always been an absolute favourite of mine.

Preheat the oven to 180°C/350°F/gas mark 4.

Peel the apples and cut out the middle core using a corer, so the rest of the apple is in one piece. Put the apples on baking (parchment) paper on a baking tray (sheet).

Melt the butter and pour a small spoonful of butter over each apple (reserving some for later). Stuff the hole in the centre of each apple with the raisins and marzipan, alternating the raisins and marzipan so they are layered inside. Finish with a layer of marzipan, allowing a little extra marzipan to come out of the top.

Pour a little more melted butter over each apple, then mix the sugar and cinnamon together and sprinkle a teaspoon of the mixture over each apple. Bake in the oven for 30 minutes.

To make the vanilla cream, in a mixing bowl whisk the eggs and sugar together, then add the vanilla seeds. In another bowl, whisk the cream until it becomes firm, then gently fold the cream into the egg mixture.

Serve the apples immediately with the vanilla cream, or with vanilla ice cream if you prefer.

Æblekage

'APPLE CAKE' WITH MACAROONS AND WHIPPED CREAM

SERVES 8

One of the 'oldies', this 'apple cake' is the kind of dessert that was traditionally made by your grandmother for your daily or weekly visits to her house.

We have almost as many apple trees in Denmark as people, therefore we are extremely creative with this wonderful fruit, using apples for both sweet and savoury dishes. My great-great-great-great-great-grandfather in fact planted the first apple trees on Tåsinge, the island that I come from.

It's a good idea to make a double portion of the apple purée, as this can also be used for an apple and bacon topping on an open sandwich, or as an accompaniment for pork chops.

FOR THE APPLE PURÉE
1kg (2¼lb) cooking apples, peeled, cored and cut into chunks
160g (5¾oz/¾ cup) raw cane sugar
2 tbsp vanilla sugar
1 vanilla pod (bean), cut into 5 pieces
pinch of cinnamon
300ml (10fl oz/1¼ cups) water

FOR THE 'CAKE'
200g (7oz) amaretti cookies (almond macaroons)
300ml (10fl oz/1¼ cups) whipping cream
4 tbsp redcurrant jelly

Place the apples in a large lidded saucepan with the sugar, vanilla sugar, vanilla pod (bean), cinnamon and the measured water – ensuring there is enough water to just cover the apples.

Over a medium heat, bring to the boil, then turn down the heat, add the lid and simmer for 30 minutes. Remove from the heat, leave to cool, then remove and discard the vanilla pod (bean) pieces.

Remove and reserve most of the water, then blend the apple mixture in a blender or food processor until thick and smooth, adding a little more of the water if needed.

Crush the amaretti cookies – you can use a mortar and pestle, or place in a sealed plastic bag and crush with a rolling pin. Whisk the cream until it is stiff and smooth.

Put a layer of the crushed amaretti cookies in the bottom of a small jam (jelly) jar. Add a thick layer of the cold apple purée, another layer of the amaretti cookies, another layer of apple and then a final layer of the amaretti cookies. Finally add a layer of the whipped cream and a dollop of the redcurrant jelly. Repeat with the rest of the jars and serve immediately.

Kirsebær Crumble

CHERRY RYE BREAD CRUMBLE

SERVES 6–8

FOR THE CHERRY FILLING
400g (14oz/3 cups) cherries, pitted
4 tbsp raspberry jam (jelly)
25g (1oz/⅛ cup) raw cane sugar
1 tbsp vanilla sugar
100ml (3½fl oz/scant ½ cup) water
1 tbsp cornflour (cornstarch)
1 tbsp lemon juice

FOR THE CRUMBLE
100g (3½oz/scant ½ cup/
    scant 1 stick) butter
100g (3½oz/scant ½ cup) coconut oil
200g (7oz) rye bread (see page 208),
    crumbled
100g (3½oz/generous 1 cup) oats
50g (1¾oz/generous ½ cup) desiccated
    coconut
160g (5¾oz/¾ cup) raw cane sugar
2 tbsp vanilla essence

TO SERVE
whipped cream or vanilla ice cream (see
    page 186)

Cherries are wondrous berries. The deeper the colour of fruits and vegetables, the richer they are in goodness. An experiment with some of our most consumed Danish ingredients became a favourite after the first time we made this cherry crumble at home. If you love cherries, and we really do – this is fantastic.

When I was little, from the age of about four, I used to love climbing trees. It was a daily activity for me and occasionally got me into big trouble. We had an enormous and very rich cherry tree in our garden, I would climb up high and sit there for hours eating cherries till my tummy ached. There was a time when I climbed so high I couldn't get back down again, and the fire brigade was called to help … or so the story goes.

In a saucepan over a medium heat bring the cherries, raspberry jam (jelly), sugar, vanilla sugar and water to the boil, then turn down the heat and simmer for 10 minutes. Add the cornflour (cornstarch) and lemon juice, stir well and set aside.

Preheat the oven to 180°C/350°F/gas mark 4.

In a saucepan, melt the butter and coconut oil. Put the crumbled rye bread, oats, desiccated coconut, sugar and vanilla essence in a mixing bowl, then pour over the melted butter and coconut oil and mix well.

Fill the bottom of an ovenproof pie dish with the cherry mixture, then carefully add the rye bread crumble mixture on top. Bake for 45 minutes, then remove from the oven and serve hot with cream or ice cream.

Farmor Kirstens Marcipankage med Banan og Daddelis

KIRSTEN'S MARZIPAN CAKE
WITH BANANA AND DATE ICE CREAM

SERVES 8

FOR THE MARZIPAN CAKE
4 eggs
200g (7oz/2 cups) icing
   (confectioner's) sugar
200g (7oz) marzipan
130g (4½oz) dark chocolate
30 whole almonds

FOR THE ICE CREAM
3 frozen bananas
9 Medjool dates
2 tbsp ground cinnamon

TO SERVE
sprigs of lemon balm

Since I was a child, if my godmother Kirsten wasn't serving rice pudding with a lump of butter and cinnamon sugar for pudding, then she would have made this marzipan cake instead, whether for a bridge lunch or a glamorous dinner party. I am thrilled that she has agreed to share this 'masterpiece'. Mamor Kirsten, as my children call her, has become exactly this, my children's grandmother, a promise she made to my mother before she died.

The wonderful and very sweet ice cream came into being when I was making a TV show, helping women become the best version of themselves. Carrie Bradshaw goes to bed with Ben & Jerry's – my girls decided to go with date ice cream!

First make the ice cream. Peel the frozen bananas, then place all the ice cream ingredients into a blender or food processor and blend well until smooth. Return to the freezer until ready to serve.

Preheat the oven to 180°C/350°F/gas mark 4.

In a large bowl, whisk 3 of the eggs together with the icing (confectioner's) sugar. In another bowl, mix the other egg with the marzipan, squeezing it through your fingers until perfectly combined (this is essential to the outcome when baking it).

Mix the sugar and marzipan mixtures together, and put it into a medium-sized springform tin (pan). Bake the base of the marzipan cake in the oven for 30 minutes, then set aside to cool.

Make a bain-marie by placing a glass or heatproof bowl over a saucepan of boiling water. Melt the chocolate in the bain-marie, then pour it over the cooled marzipan base and smooth out.

Place the whole almonds in a bowl of boiling water for a minute, then drain and remove the skins. Decorate the top of the cake with the almonds and serve with the ice cream and lemon balm.

Chokoladekage
STICKY CHOCOLATE PUDDING

SERVES 6–8

FOR THE CHOCOLATE PUDDING
100g (3½oz/scant ½ cup/1 stick) butter
2 eggs
250g (9oz/1¼ cups) raw cane sugar
100g (3½oz/¾ cup) plain (all-purpose)
    flour
½ tsp baking powder
5 tbsp high-quality cacao powder
½ tsp pink Himalayan salt or sea salt
1 vanilla pod (bean), cut in half and
    seeds scraped out, or 1 tbsp
    vanilla extract
50g (1¾oz/2½ tbsp) maple syrup
zest of 1 orange
juice of ½ an orange

FOR THE RASPBERRY COULIS
200g (7oz) raspberries
2 tbsp honey

I have such clear memories of our electric hand mixer as it was used almost every day of my childhood, and if you have one then this pudding is very simple to make.

Sticky and gooey, this pudding is fabulous for any occasion, whether you are having guests over for tea and card games, or a smart dinner party. It will also be a real treat for your children, any time, any day.

I first tasted this many years ago when an old family nanny, Rikke, who has the sweetest tooth I have ever come across, made it for us. I couldn't speak for a while … speechless by chocolate. This cake will always be a girl's best friend!

Preheat the oven to 180°C/350°F/gas mark 4. Line a loose-bottomed 23cm (9 inch) cake tin.

Melt the butter and set aside to cool. Using an electric whisk, whisk together the eggs and sugar until they become white and creamy. Mix the flour, baking powder, cacao powder, salt, vanilla seeds and maple syrup into the egg and sugar mixture. Add the orange zest and juice and stir again well, then add the cooled butter and stir again.

Pour the mixture into the cake tin and bake in the oven for 20 minutes. The cake may seem a little undercooked, but it should be gooey and will glue together when it cools down.

While the pudding cooks, make the raspberry coulis by putting the raspberries and honey into a blender and blending until smooth.

Serve the pudding with a good drizzle of raspberry coulis.

TIP
— You can also make a great mint-chocolate pudding, which is perfect on a winter's afternoon with a cup of steaming hot chocolate (see page 245). Just replace the orange juice and zest with 1 tsp of peppermint oil.

Chapter Seven

Bread, Bakes, Sweet Treats and Drinks

Rugbrød

TRADITIONAL RYE BREAD

MAKES 3 LOAVES

FOR THE RYE BREAD MOTHER

50ml (2fl oz/scant ¼ cup) buttermilk

60g (2oz/½ cup) whole rye flour

2.5g (¾ tsp) fresh yeast

FOR THE RYE BREAD DOUGH

750ml (1⅓ pints/3 cups) warm water

1 x quantity of the Rye Bread Mother
(see above)

2 tbsp coarse sea salt

300g (10½oz/2 cups) cracked rye
kernels

250g (9oz/1½ cups) wheat kernels

250g (9oz/1½ cups) linseeds
(flaxseeds)

250g (9oz/scant 2 cups) sunflower seeds

125g (4½oz/¾ cup) buckwheat groats

750g (1lb 10oz/6 cups) wheat flour

500g (1lb 2oz/4 cups) rye flour

FOR THE BAKED RYE BREAD

750ml (1⅓ pints/3 cups) lukewarm water

25g (1oz/scant 3 tbsp) fresh yeast

500g (1lb 2oz/4 cups) rye flour

oil, to brush

This recipe is a marriage between my late mother's recipe and the recipe of one of her best friends, Audrey, who helped me to find this original. There are probably as many variations of rye bread in Denmark as there are wheat breads in Europe. In the good old days, you would start with a 'rye bread mother', which would be a large tennis ball-size portion of the last unbaked rye bread you had made, kept for next time. These 'mothers' have passed down from one generation to another – I don't recall when our one got lost, but it was probably around the time we moved to England

It is still possible to make your 'mother' from scratch, but it does take a couple of extra days. I hope this becomes a regular tradition in your home, and that you experience the magic of passing a *rugbrødsmor* on to the next generation – happy baking.

If you don't already have the 'rye bread mother', mix all the rye bread mother ingredients together in a bowl and leave in a warm place for 24 hours covered with a clean tea towel.

To make the rye bread dough, mix all the rye bread ingredients together and knead very well, then leave for 24 hours.

When the dough has rested, mix the measured water, fresh yeast and rye flour for the baked rye bread together. When combined, mix well into your rye bread dough. Reserve 150g (5½oz) of the bread dough and place in an airtight container (this will be your next 'rye bread mother'). This will keep in the fridge for about 6 weeks.

Divide the rest of the mixture between 3 loaf tins (pans), about 23 x 13cm (9 x 5 inches), and leave in a warm place to rise for 6 hours.

When ready to bake, preheat the oven to 180°C/350°F/gas mark 4. Brush the tops of the loaves with oil. Bake the loaves on the bottom shelf of your oven for 90 minutes. Remove from the loaf tins (pans) and leave to cool. This bread also freezes well.

Nøddebrød

NUT BREAD

MAKES 1 LOAF

250g (9oz/1¾ cups) whole raw almonds

250g (9oz/1⅔ cups) pumpkin seeds,
   plus 50g (1¾oz/⅓ cup)

150g (5½oz/1 cup) sunflower seeds

50g (1¾oz/scant ⅓ cup) golden linseeds
   (golden flaxseeds)

50g (1¾oz/scant ⅓ cup) brown linseeds
   (brown flaxseeds)

20g (¾oz/2 tbsp) chia seeds

30g (1¼oz/scant ½ cup)
   psyllium husks

½ tbsp pink Himalayan salt or sea salt

600ml (1 pint/2½ cups) cold water

It takes quite a lot of time to make the traditional rye bread (opposite), and although it is so worth it, if you cannot find the time, here is a great alternative.

This completely delicious version of Danish rye bread is gluten free, dairy free and wheat free, which I know means a lot to many people. When I make this bread I make a double batch and freeze it in slices, so I always have it handy. It also makes a great alternative to rye bread for the traditional open Danish sandwiches (see pages 58–9).

Blend the almonds and 250g (9oz/1⅔ cups) of the pumpkin seeds together to make a fine flour.

In a large bowl, mix together the almond and pumpkin flour, the extra 50g (1¾oz/⅓ cup) of pumpkin seeds and the rest of the ingredients. Mix well until combined and leave for 1 hour in a warm place, covered in clingfilm (plastic wrap).

Preheat the oven to 180°C/350°F/gas mark 4.

Place the dough in a 23 x 13cm (9 x 5 inch) loaf tin (pan) and bake for 75 minutes. Remove from the tin (pan) and leave to cool.

Previous pages, from left to right: Rugbrød, Nøddebrød.

Mors Mad Brød

MY MOTHER'S FOOD BREAD

MAKES 1 FOOD BREAD

500ml (18fl oz/2 cups) warm water
50g (1¾oz/5 tbsp) fresh yeast
125g (4½oz/generous ½ cup/1 stick)
   butter, cut into chunks
1 egg
100g (3½oz/¾ cup) sesame seeds
3 tsp pink Himalayan salt or sea salt
1 shallot, finely chopped
1 stick of celery, finely chopped
1 small carrot, grated
2 tsp lemon juice
1 tsp soy sauce
850g (1lb 15oz/scant 7 cups) plain
   (all-purpose) flour

When my darling godmother, Kirsten, asked me recently if I remembered my mother's savoury food bread, which I had last had when I was 11, I was instantly hit by a recollection of the smell and flavour of these buns. Now that I've followed my mother's recipe, the aroma and taste of my food bread were identical to my imagination and it felt like my mother was in the room with me again. How precious and special to feel like someone passed is with us again and again.

In a large bowl, mix together the warm water and the yeast until combined. Add the rest of the ingredients but only half of the flour. Mix and knead until well combined. Gradually add as much of the rest of the flour as the dough will take.

Place the dough in a large bowl, cover with a clean tea towel and leave in a warm place to rise for 1 hour.

Divide the dough into 15 to 20 round buns and place them close together on a baking tray (sheet). Leave to rise for 30 minutes.

Meanwhile, preheat the oven to 200°C/400°F/gas mark 6.

Bake the bread for 40 minutes. It is quite delicious either warm or cold.

Fødselsdagsboller

DANISH BIRTHDAY BUNS

MAKES 12 BUNS

250ml (8½fl oz/1 cup) warm water
50g (1¾oz/5 tbsp) fresh yeast
500g (1lb 2oz/4 cups) plain
  (all-purpose) flour
pinch of salt
50g (1¾oz/¼ cup) raw cane sugar
1 tsp ground cardamom
1 egg

These buns are quite simply to die for – freshly baked, served warm and topped with half-melted 'tooth butter' – a very Danish expression. We love our butter, so much so that there needs to be enough butter, thickly spread on the bread, to show your front teeth marks when you bite into it.

When I make these buns I normally make a double batch and freeze some, as they are great for an easy weekend breakfast.

The dough (excluding the sugar) can also be used to wrap around a frankfurter sausage and baked to make delicious sausage rolls for picnics or *pølser med snobrød*. This alternative Danish hot dog is wonderful to make on Midsummer's Eve, although the classic is not to be missed if you visit Denmark, as hot dog stands feature on practically every street corner, like fresh pretzel stands in New York.

Susan, the mother of my children's last nanny, Cecilie, makes their favourite birthday buns. I have used her base and added my favourite bakery spice.

Pour the warm water into a large bowl, then add the yeast, stirring as you add it. Mix well, then add the rest of the ingredients and stir until combined. Knead thoroughly, then leave in a bowl in a dark, warm place, covered with a clean tea towel, to rise for 30 minutes.

Divide the dough into 12 balls and roll each bun in your hands to make a rounded ball. Leave to rise for another 30 minutes.

Preheat the oven to 220°C/425°F/gas mark 7. Line a baking tray (sheet) with baking (parchment) paper.

Place the buns, spread out, on the baking tray (sheet) and bake in the oven for 10–12 minutes.

Remove the buns from the oven, leave to cool for 10 minutes, then cut in half and spread thickly with butter. Lastly, put a small flag stick into each bun if you are celebrating a birthday.

Kanelsnegle

CINNAMON BUNS

MAKES 16–20 BUNS

FOR THE BUNS

500ml (18fl oz/2 cups) milk

125g (4½oz/1 cup) icing (confectioner's) sugar

60g (2oz/¼ cup/½ stick) butter

50g (1¾oz/5 tbsp) fresh yeast

1kg (2¼lb/8 cups) plain (all-purpose) flour, plus extra to dust

1 tsp ground cardamom

2 eggs

FOR THE FILLING

175g (6¼oz/¾ cup/1½ sticks) butter, softened

250g (9oz/1¼ cups) raw cane sugar

3 tbsp ground cinnamon

Every year my grandparents would come and stay with my sister Duddi and I when our parents went shooting around Europe for a month. The first thing Granny made as soon as she arrived was a ginormous portion of cinnamon buns. My sister and I would eat these every day when we got back from school, and also – if we were lucky – for breakfast. Granny baked these again just before she left and froze them in smaller batches, which is such a good idea as these buns truly are the most heavenly snack for children, both big and small.

In a large saucepan, gently heat the milk until it is warm, not hot, then add the icing (confectioner's) sugar and butter. Remove from the heat, stir to combine, then leave to cool.

Once cool, add the yeast and stir well, then slowly add the flour and cardamom, stirring well. Whisk the eggs, then add to the saucepan and stir well to combine. Remove the bun dough from the saucepan and knead well, then cover with a clean tea towel and leave in a dark place for 1 hour to rise.

Lightly flour your work surface. Roll the dough mixture out into a large rectangle about 1cm (½ inch) thick.

Mix the ingredients for the filling together, then spread the filling all over the top of the dough rectangle. Roll up, starting from one end, so that it resembles a jam roly-poly cake or Swiss roll, then cut into 2cm (¾ inch) thick slices. Spread the slices out on baking (parchment) paper on a baking tray (sheet) and allow to rise for another 30 minutes.

Meanwhile, preheat the oven to 200°C/400°F/gas mark 6.

Bake the cinnamon buns for 10–15 minutes until golden brown. Enjoy warm from the oven, or cold, with a cup of tea or coffee. These also freeze well.

Brunkager

CINNAMON CHRISTMAS COOKIES

MAKES ABOUT 50 COOKIES

120g (4oz/scant 1 cup) whole raw
    almonds
250g (9oz/1¼ cups) raw cane sugar
200g (7oz/generous ½ cup)
    golden syrup (light corn syrup)
250g (9oz/generous 1 cup/2¼ sticks)
    butter, cubed
2 tbsp ground cinnamon
1 tbsp ground cardamom
2 tsp ground ginger
1 tsp allspice
2 tbsp ground cloves
500g (1lb 2oz/4 cups) plain (all-purpose)
    flour
1 tbsp bicarbonate of soda (baking soda)
1 tbsp water
2 tbsp orange peel

The happiest times of a child's life has to include birthdays and Christmases, and I remember clearly both my grandmother and my mother making these cookies at those special times. In Denmark, these celebrations have the same ingredients and wonderful smells, year after year, generation after generation, century after century. We fly our flag high, proud to be Danish, lucky to have been born with such great family *hygge* values and traditions – it really is no wonder that Denmark and its people are voted the happiest in the world year after year.

Place the almonds in boiling water and leave for a couple of minutes, then drain and remove the skins. Roughly chop and set aside.

Place the sugar, syrup and butter in a saucepan and bring just to a simmer, then remove from the heat.

In a large bowl, mix the spices, flour and chopped almonds together. In a small bowl, mix together the bicarbonate of soda (baking soda) and water, then add to the spice mix. Pour in the sugar syrup, add the orange peel and mix well. Leave to cool.

Divide the cookie dough into 2 long, fat sausage shapes. You can either make the cookies now, or cover with clingfilm (plastic wrap) and keep in the fridge until ready to use. The mixture can easily keep in the fridge for a few weeks, but will need to be removed from the fridge a couple of hours before you want to bake.

Preheat the oven to 200°C/400°F/gas mark 6.

Cut the dough into thin slices or roll out thinly and cut out shapes with cookie cutters. Bake the cookies for 5–7 minutes until nicely browned.

Kagemand

BIRTHDAY CAKEMAN OR CAKEWOMAN

SERVES 10–12

This is a must for every Danish child's birthday. It originally comes from the island of Fyn, which is also called 'Brunsviger', and there are many different variations. Being such a fan of coconut, my version of this traditional birthday cake reflects this love. It is very typical in Denmark, if you don't bake, to order your child's birthday cake from your local bakery.

FOR THE CAKE

250ml (8½fl oz/1 cup) warm water

50g (1¾oz/5 tbsp) fresh yeast

500g (1lb 2oz/4 cups) plain
   (all-purpose) flour

pinch of salt

50g (1¾oz/¼ cup) raw cane sugar

1 tsp ground cardamom

1 egg

Pour the warm water into a large bowl, then add the yeast, stirring as you add it. Mix well, then add the rest of the ingredients and stir until combined. Knead thoroughly, then leave in a bowl in a dark, warm place, covered with a clean tea towel, to rise for 30 minutes.

When risen, form the dough into the shape of a boy or a girl and place on a piece of baking (parchment) paper on a baking tray (sheet). Leave to rise for another 20 minutes. Preheat the oven to 200°C/400°F/gas mark 6.

FOR THE TOPPING

200g (7oz/scant 1 cup/1¾ sticks) butter

200g (7oz/generous ½ cup) molasses

3 tbsp desiccated coconut

2 tbsp ground cinnamon

Bake the cakeman/woman for 10 minutes, then remove from the oven. Leave the oven on.

To make the topping, in a bowl soften (but do not melt) the butter. Add the rest of the ingredients and stir well until all combined.

TO DECORATE

Long sweety strings/laces
   (candy threads)

gummy bears

chocolate beans (I use Smarties)

liquorice

Or any other candy you adore!

With a fork, make small holes all over the top of the cake and then pour the topping over the cakeman/woman – it will seep into the holes. Return to the oven and bake for another 5 minutes, then remove and leave to cool slightly.

Decorate the cakeman/woman using your favourite sweets. This is most delicious when served warm.

Havregryn og Vanillekiks/ Kammerjunkere

VANILLA AND OAT COOKIES

**MAKES 24 COOKIES
OR 40 KAMMERJUNKERE**

150g (5½oz/1⅔ cups) oats

150g (5½oz/2 cups) desiccated coconut

200g (7oz/1½ cups) whole raw almonds,
  chopped

1 egg

2 tsp vanilla sugar

1 fresh vanilla pod (bean), halved
  and seeds scraped out

250g (9oz/1¼ cups) raw cane sugar

1 tbsp baking powder

250g (9oz/generous 1 cup/2¼ sticks)
  butter, softened

I loved going to kindergarten in Denmark. One of my favourite things to do, when the day was over, was going to visit my oldest friend Sofie, who I met at the doctor's when I was one-and-a-half, because we were both having our jabs. Her mother started talking to my mother because I screamed so loudly! We have been friends ever since. When the playdate was at her house, we would always have milk with chocolate powder mixed in and two delicious biscuits (cookies) each. My love of biscuits (cookies) started then, and continues to this day. These oat cookies are a real family favourite, and we also used them in the *koldskål* recipe (cold buttermilk soup, see page 188).

Mix all the ingredients together in a large bowl until combined. Put in a cool place for a few hours or even overnight.

When ready to bake, preheat the oven to 200°C/400°F/gas mark 6.

Shape the dough into small balls (about 24 if making cookies, and 40 if making *kammerjunkere*) and press flat with your finger or thumb. Place spread out on a baking tray (sheet) and bake for 20 minutes.

These will keep for a few weeks in an airtight container, and the cookies are lovely with a cup of tea or hot chocolate. The *kammerjunkere* are also fantastic with *koldskål* (cold buttermilk soup, see page 188).

Sund Slik

HEALTHY CANDY

It's very interesting how 'healthy candy', also known today as protein balls, bars, sticks etc. has become so popular.

As children we would have 'healthy candy' in our packed lunches, for example rye bread with fig sticks on top. Back then it would be a disappointment to be served healthy candy for pudding, but today my children, friends and family have a newfound love for these nutritious and delicious bites, great for any time of day.

I recall so clearly seeing these bites in bakeries or health food shops, and never realized how easy and fun they are to make. They have existed with such popularity in Denmark for as long as I can remember, and they are so good that cravings for artificial sugary confections will disappear.

Figenstang

FIG STICKS

MAKES ABOUT 12 STICKS

200g (7oz/1⅓ cups) dried figs,
   stalks removed
100g (3½oz/⅔ cup) pitted Medjool dates
100g (3½oz/⅔ cup) whole raw almonds
50g (1¾oz/¼ cup) coconut oil, melted
2 tbsp honey
50g (1¾oz/generous ½ cup)
   desiccated coconut

In a blender or food processor, blend all the ingredients except for the desiccated coconut until combined.

Place the desiccated coconut on a small plate.

Take out a large spoonful of the mixture and shape it into a small sausage or stick shape, then roll in the desiccated coconut. Repeat with the rest of the mixture. Put in the fridge to set.

Abrikosskiver

APRICOT SLICES

MAKES ABOUT 12 SLICES

250g (9oz/1½ cups) dried apricots
100g (3½oz/⅔ cup) pitted Medjool dates
100g (3½oz/¾ cup) roasted hazelnuts,
   without the skin
50g (1¾oz/generous ½ cup) desiccated
   coconut
70g (2½oz/⅓ cup) coconut oil, melted
2 tbsp honey or maple syrup
4 tbsp cocoa powder (optional)

In a blender or food processor, blend all the ingredients together until combined.

Press into a small tin. Leave to set in the fridge, then take out and cut into slices or squares.

Hindbærstykker
RASPBERRY PIECES OR BALLS

MAKES 12 PIECES OR 18 BALLS

200g (7oz/1½ cups) whole raw almonds

100g (3½oz/1¼ cups) desiccated
  coconut

100g (3½oz/½ cup) coconut oil, melted

50g (1¾oz) dried raspberries

4 tbsp honey or maple syrup

raspberry powder, to dust

In a blender or food processor, blend all the ingredients together
until combined.

Shape the mixture into 12 small pieces or 18 balls, dust with
raspberry powder and place in the fridge to set.

Kakao Havrekugler
COCOA OAT BALLS

MAKES 18 BALLS

100g (3½oz/1 cup) rolled oats,
  plus extra to roll

150g (5½oz/¾ cup) coconut oil, melted

150g (5½oz/1 cup) pitted Medjool dates

40g (1½oz/⅓ cup) good-quality cocoa
  powder

40g (1½oz/⅓ cup) cacao nibs

In a blender or food processor, blend all the ingredients together
except for the extra oats until combined.

Sprinkle the oats for rolling onto a plate. Form the oat mixture into
18 small balls and roll each ball lightly in the oats.

Karamel

TOFFEE

We are a nation with a very sweet tooth. Sometimes our taste for sweets comes in the shape of very salty liquorice, which is often a shock when a stranger to liquorice tastes this remarkably salty black thing for the first time. It is probably the same as when a Dane first tastes Marmite. The facial squint says it all…

Lakridskaramel

LIQUORICE TOFFEE

MAKES 20 PIECES

180g (6½oz/¾ cup) raw cane sugar
140g (5oz/⅔ cup/1⅓ sticks) butter
1 x 400g (14oz) can sweetened
  condensed milk
150ml (5fl oz/⅔ cup) liquorice syrup
pinch of salt
liquorice powder, for dusting

Line a small tin (pan) with baking (parchment) paper.

Place the sugar, butter, condensed milk, liquorice syrup and salt in a saucepan over a low heat, allowing the ingredients to melt together. Once melted, bring to a simmer and simmer for 15 minutes, stirring regularly.

Pour the toffee into the tin (pan) and place in the fridge to cool for 30 minutes. Take the toffee out of the tin (pan), cut into 20 squares, and dust each square with the liquorice powder.

Place in a glass container to store, or wrap in clear sweet wrappers. I like to serve these cold from the fridge or freezer.

Knäck

SWEDISH CHRISTMAS TOFFEE

MAKES 20 PIECES

180g (6½oz/¾ cup) raw cane
  sugar
140g (5oz/⅔ cup/1⅓ sticks)
  butter
1 x 400g (14oz) can of sweetened
  condensed milk
150g (5½oz/scant ½ cup)
  golden syrup (light corn syrup)
50g (1¾oz/⅓ cup) chopped
  almonds

Place the sugar in a saucepan and melt over a low heat. When it's all melted and golden, add the butter, sweetened condensed milk and syrup, stirring well, then let the ingredients gently simmer over a low heat for about 10 minutes. Add the almonds, stir well, then allow to cool a little.

Pour into miniature paper cake cases (mini candy cups), then put in the fridge until ready to serve.

Chokolade Pebermynter

HOMEMADE AFTER-DINNER MINTS

MAKES ABOUT 20 MINTS

FOR THE AFTER-DINNER MINTS

350g (12oz/3 cups) icing
   (confectioner's) sugar

1 tsp lemon juice

½ tsp peppermint oil

1 pasteurized egg white

100g (3½oz) good-quality chocolate,
   milk, dark or even sea salt

These treats are especially good after a meal, the perfect time to have something sweet. I have also made these flavoured with orange blossom and lavender oil and they were divine – simply substitute the peppermint oil for (edible) lavender or orange blossom oil.

Mix 250g (9oz/generous 2 cups) of the icing (confectioner's) sugar together with the lemon juice, peppermint oil and the egg white. Continue to add the icing (confectioner's) sugar until the peppermint mixture is very thick and firm (you may not need to use all of it).

Make small balls out of the peppermint mixture, then gently press them flat into circular shapes.

Make a bain-marie by placing a glass or heatproof bowl over a saucepan of boiling water and slowly melt the chocolate in the bain-marie. Carefully spread a bit of chocolate on the centre of each mint, or cover the whole top surface.

Put into the fridge or freezer and allow to cool and set completely.

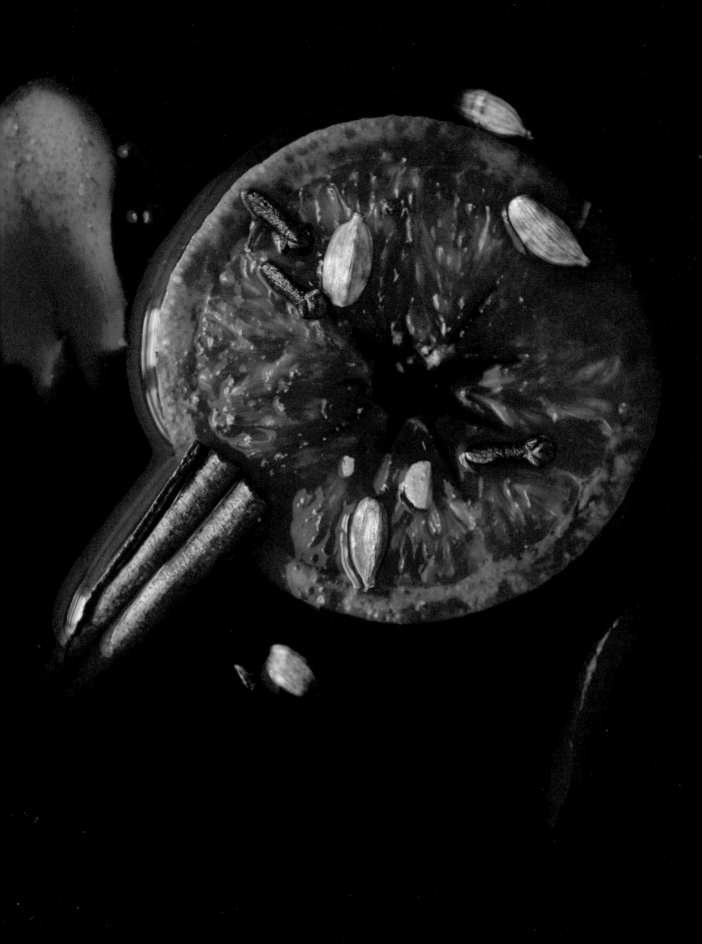

Rød Gløgg

RED MULLED WINE

SERVES 8

1.5 litres (2½ pints/6 cups) red wine
18 whole cloves
12 cardamom pods
2 cinnamon sticks
1 whole orange, sliced
3cm (1¼ inch) long thin slice
   of fresh ginger
200g (7oz/1 cup) raw cane sugar
300ml (10fl oz/1¼ cups) sweet vermouth
200ml (7fl oz/generous ¾ cup) vodka
200g (7oz/generous 2 cups) flaked
   almonds
200g (7oz/scant 1¼ cups) raisins

I believe in 'any excuse' for a glass of mulled wine, not just when the temperature outside is below freezing. In Denmark we start serving mulled wine in November, as soon as winter has properly stepped into season, and don't just keep it for Christmas and the ski season. Although skiing holidays would not be the same without mulled wine.

This red mulled wine is lovely served with vanilla and oat cookies (see page 226) or cinnamon Christmas cookies (see page 222), and will really warm you deep into your soul.

Put the red wine, cloves, cardamom pods, cinnamon sticks, orange slices, ginger and sugar in a large saucepan and allow to stand overnight (or for at least 12 hours) with the lid on.

The next day, add the vermouth and vodka and bring to a gentle boil. After simmering for 10 minutes, strain through a sieve to remove all the spices and orange pieces, then add the almonds and raisins and gently simmer for a further 10 minutes.

Serve in glasses or mugs, with teaspoons for easy eating of the raisins and almonds.

Hvid Gløgg
WHITE MULLED WINE

SERVES 8

1.5 litres (2½ pints/6 cups)
  white wine
10 whole cloves
8 cardamom pods
3 star anise
2 tbsp candied orange peel
200ml (7fl oz/generous ¾ cup)
  elderflower cordial
160g (5¾oz/¾ cup) raw cane sugar
2 cinnamon sticks
1 whole vanilla pod (bean), halved
  lengthways
3cm (1¼ inch) long thin slice
  of fresh ginger
peel of one organic lemon
  (keep the lemon flesh for thin
  slices in each cup)
200ml (7fl oz/generous ¾ cup) white rum
200ml (7fl oz/generous ¾ cup) Cointreau
200g (7oz/generous 2 cups) flaked
  almonds
200g (7oz/1¼ cups) sultanas
  (golden raisins)

I only tasted white *gløgg* for the first time about five years ago. It was in the hotel lobby of my favourite hotel in Copenhagen and was such an unusual taste experience, having only ever had red *gløgg* before, that it was really quite addictive, and I think I had five glasses before I could stop. Here is my version of that memorable drink.

Put the white wine, cloves, cardamom pods, star anise, candied orange peel, elderflower cordial, sugar, cinnamon sticks, vanilla pod, ginger and lemon peel in a large saucepan and allow to stand overnight (or for at least 12 hours) with the lid on.

The next day, add the rum and Cointreau and bring to a gentle boil. After simmering for 10 minutes, strain through a sieve to remove all the spices and lemon peel, then add the almonds and sultanas (golden raisins) and gently simmer for a further 10 minutes.

Serve in glasses or mugs with a slice of lemon, and a teaspoon for easy eating of the sultanas (golden raisins) and almonds.

Varm Kakao med Appelsinsirup

HOT CHOCOLATE WITH ORANGE SYRUP

SERVES 6

FOR THE HOT CHOCOLATE

300g (10½oz) finest dark chocolate
  (about 60–70% cocoa solids)
1 litre (1¾ pints/4 cups) milk, at room
  temperature
100g (3½oz/½ cup) raw cane sugar
  (to your taste, less if you prefer)

TO TOP

200ml (7fl oz/generous ¾ cup)
  whipping cream

FOR THE ORANGE SYRUP

100ml (3½fl oz/scant ½ cup) water
150g (5½oz/¾ cup) raw cane sugar
3 strips of orange peel
1 tbsp cornflour (cornstarch)
juice of 2 sweet oranges, pips removed
60ml (2¼fl oz/¼ cup) Grand Marnier
  or Cointreau
1 tbsp unsalted butter (optional)

One of my favourite things around Christmas time is hot chocolate. Sitting by the fireplace, reading Christmas stories with my children, drinking hot chocolate with Christmas melodies playing in the background. I also adore going to Paris at Christmas time, especially to go and have a hot chocolate at Angelina's Café, which opened in 1903, its speciality being hot chocolate. Having visited countless times, I was inspired to create my own sumptuous hot chocolate recipe, which I think is the most delicious ever.

First whip the cream for the topping until stiff.

To make the orange syrup, bring the measured water to a gentle boil and add the sugar and orange peel. Mix well and keep simmering until the sugar has dissolved.

Slowly sieve in the cornflour (cornstarch) and mix well. Add the orange juice, Grand Marnier and butter, if you wish, and simmer gently until the mixture thickens, then turn off the heat.

Make a bain-marie by placing a glass or heatproof bowl over a saucepan of boiling water. Slowly melt the chocolate in the top of the bain-marie. Once it has melted completely, gradually add the milk, stirring all the time, combining the chocolate and milk completely before adding more. The chocolate needs to have melted completely before you add the milk or the mixture will separate.

Pour the hot chocolate from the bowl into a saucepan and heat through. Serve immediately in mugs with the orange syrup (or you can use peppermint syrup if you prefer) and whipped cream.

Saftevand

CORDIALS AND FLAVOURED WATERS

'Playing all day every day' is a huge part of the Danish mentality. We do not really start school before we are about six or seven years old, and most of what we learn is through play – in fact this continues well into the teenage years. A childhood in Denmark is a very wholesome and endearing experience.

Through all this playing comes great thirst, and what is more fabulous than quenching your thirst with fresh cordials, made in season, and refreshing flavoured waters, enough to keep you quenched all year round. These are my favourite waters, but have fun experimenting with different combos.

Hyldeblomst Saft

ELDERFLOWER CORDIAL

MAKES 2 LITRES (2½ PINTS)

1kg (2¼lb/5 cups) raw cane sugar
2 litres (3½ pints/8 cups) filtered water
4 large lemons, thinly sliced
50 newly cut elderflower heads,
   well rinsed

Put the sugar and water in a large saucepan. Heat slowly over a low heat and allow the sugar to melt completely, then add the lemon slices and elderflower heads. Stir well, then turn off the heat. Place the saucepan in a cool place and stir every few hours for 4 days, then filter through a muslin (cheesecloth). Pour into sterilized bottles and store in a cool, dark place. This will keep for 7–10 days.

When serving, dilute 1 part cordial to 3 parts filtered water.

Hyldebær Saft

ELDERBERRY CORDIAL

MAKES 2 LITRES (2½ PINTS)

4kg (9lb) elderberries
2 litres (3½ pints/8 cups) filtered water
1.5kg (3lb 5oz/7½ cups) raw cane sugar
1 lemon, quartered

Put the elderberries into a large saucepan and add the water. Over a low heat bring just to the boil, then allow to gently simmer for about 30 minutes. Pour the elderberries through an old muslin (cheesecloth), then pour just the juice back into the saucepan. Add the sugar and lemon and simmer for another 15–20 minutes, by which time the sugar should have completely melted. Pour into sterilized bottles and store in a cool, dark place. This will keep for 7–10 days.

When serving, dilute 1 part cordial to 3 parts filtered water.

Hindbær Saft

RASPBERRY CORDIAL

MAKES 2 LITRES (2½ PINTS)

4kg (9lb) raspberries
2 litres (3½ pints/8 cups) filtered water
1.8kg (4lb/9 cups) raw cane sugar
juice of 1 lemon

Place the raspberries and 500ml (18fl oz/2 cups) of water in a large saucepan. Bring to the boil over a low heat, then simmer for 10 minutes. Using a potato masher, mash the raspberries well. Add the sugar, lemon juice and remaining water, bring back to the boil, then simmer for 30 minutes. Allow to cool, then pour through a muslin (cheesecloth). Pour into a couple of sterilized bottles and store in the fridge. This will keep for 2 weeks.

When serving, dilute 1 part cordial to 3 parts filtered water.

Agurk Vand

CUCUMBER-INFUSED WATER

MAKES 1 LITRE (1¾ PINTS)

1 cucumber
1 litre (1¾ pints/4 cups) fresh
    filtered water
handful of ice cubes

Using a vegetable peeler, take approximately 20 long slices from the length of the cucumber, using all the skin and the first few outer layers (not the seeded centre).

Put the water, cucumber and ice into a jug and drink straight away, or keep in the fridge until you are ready to serve.

Jordbær, Citron og Ingefær Vand

STRAWBERRY, LEMON & GINGER-
INFUSED WATER

MAKES 1 LITRE (1¾ PINTS)

200g (7oz/1 cup) strawberries
4cm (1½ inch) piece of ginger
1 small lemon
1 litre (1¾ pints/4 cups) fresh
    filtered water
handful of ice cubes

Thinly slice the strawberries, ginger and lemon.

Put the strawberry, ginger and lemon slices into a jug, add the water and ice. Drink straight away or keep in the fridge until you are ready to serve.

Brændenælde Te

NETTLE TEA

SERVES 2–4

FOR THE NETTLE TEA
100g (3½oz) stinging nettle leaves
600ml (1 pint/2½ cups) boiling water

In Denmark we don't see nettles as horrid weeds to stay away from, but rather as one of nature's amazing ingredients. Nettle soup is an old family favourite, and this tea is not to be missed. Do take into consideration the remarkable health benefits of nettles, and allow me to share a few I believe in: nettles boost the immune system, support the adrenals (which I need as mine are often in overdrive!), relieve period pains and bloating, reduce inflammation, relieve nausea and help constipation, to name a few.

If you want to be able to drink nettle tea regularly, pick extra nettle leaves and dry them, then make your own homemade tea bags from them.

Wearing thick gloves, go out into the woods and pluck about 100g (3½oz) of stinging nettle leaves, bring them home and wash really well.

Place the nettles in a teapot, pour over the boiling water, then strain and enjoy.

NOTES
– Ideally pick the tips and young leaves of the nettles, and don't pick them once they start to form flowers.
– Just one note of caution, if you are pregnant or on certain medication then nettle tea may not be suitable for you. Please check with your doctor first.

Is Te

ICED TEA

SERVES 6

FOR THE ICED TEA
300ml (10fl oz/1¼ cups) water
4 Earl Grey tea bags
100g (3½oz/½ cup) raw cane sugar
1 tbsp vanilla sugar
juice of 2 lemons
900ml (1½ pints/3¾ cups) cold water
lots of ice

What is there not to love about iced tea? I became particularly fond of it when I started travelling to Thailand, as the Thais make an awesome iced Thai tea! It will always be on the top of my list and one of the first things I enjoy when I arrive in Thailand.

This iced tea is inspired by a flavour I came across at the age of about ten, when my best male friend Ulrich, who I have been friends with since I was born, started drinking iced tea in large quantities. I can't wait to make this one for him...

Boil the water, then leave it to cool slightly. Put the Earl Grey tea bags in a large, heatproof jug and pour over the not-quite boiling water.

Allow to brew for 3–4 minutes, then remove the tea bags. Add the sugar and stir well so it melts completely. Then add the vanilla sugar and lemon juice and stir well.

Pour over the cold water and add lots of ice. Serve immediately.

NOTE
– Do not use boiling water as it can damage the tea leaves' fantastic health benefits. For the above iced tea, use water at a maximum temperature of 85°C/185°F; for white and green teas use water at around 70°C/158°F.

Index

Acknowledgements

My first and greatest thanks goes to my three beloved children – Alexander, Josephine and Nicholas – for their incredible patience during the writing of this cookbook. Thank you for always being open to tasting my new recipes – your fantastic opinions, of course, I treasure the most.

A lifelong thank you goes to my amazing parents, who tragically are no longer with us. Every day of my childhood they inspired me, in nature collecting fresh produce, and in the kitchen cooking a great variety of dishes, everything always made from scratch. They would involve my sister Duddi and I from as early as I can remember, inspiring me to do the same with my children – my favourite times always.

Thank you darling Mormor, for everything you are and have been to me, and for the most old-fashioned dishes, which could easily have got lost with time, but your passion kept them alive. You and Morfar hold one of the most special places in my heart. I thank my darling sister, Duddi, and Nikolaj for opening your hearts to me and seeing potential dreams come true, reading through my manuscript, and for our children, whose love for each other makes everything possible. Thank you to my beloved Godmother Kirsten, and Caroline, Barbara and Estelle for being four of the wisest women I know, always supporting me in the most grounded, honest, centered and correct way – I am so lucky to have you in my life.

I want to thank all of my darling friends, you all deserve a mention, but I know your love of privacy. It is, however, impossible not to mention Ulle-Far, Søs, Anastasia, Julie, Sam and Thomas – you have been such an enormous source of strength for me, unconditionally, and especially through the last weeks of my father's life, when working on my book at such a painful time would have been impossible without your love and support. Thank you for giving me strength.

My heartfelt thanks go to Charles Finch, 'Darling Finchy', had you not believed in me, I don't think I would have had the faith to approach my literary agent PFD. Caroline Michel and Tim Bates – thank you for giving me the chance to show you who I am and share my life's great passion for every aspect of food and love, helping to bring *hygge* into my cooking.

I thank you Jacqui, you are a very special lady, my soul connects deeply with yours, and I could not have wished for a more perfect publisher. I appreciate and deeply respect your extraordinary brilliance, and I thank you for believing in me and making one of my biggest dreams come true.

Thank you also to the incredible team of people who helped me to make this book possible – Mikkel Karstad, Lisa Linder, Claire, Charlotte and Fritha – it's been a truly remarkable journey. Even the sun shone on us on the days it was meant to rain – I think my Daddy played a big role here...

Author Biography

Caroline Fleming has a huge following as a model, TV presenter, reality TV star, lifestyle guru and businesswoman. She is one of the leading stars of the reality TV show *Ladies of London*, which is shown in 22 countries. Her role in the series is very much the home-maker in the kitchen, and she is a lifestyle mentor for many of her fans. She has also recently developed her own kitchenware range.

When working as a model, Caroline realized that the better she ate, the better her complexion was, the higher her energy levels were and the better she felt overall. A mother of three, here she shares her family recipes so you can cook and be happy the Danish way. Caroline has already published three best-selling cookery books in Denmark, but this will be her first published in the English language.